ONE YEAR OF LIVING WITH COVID-19

AN ASSESSMENT OF HOW ADB MEMBERS FOUGHT THE PANDEMIC IN 2020

MAY 2021

ADB

ASIAN DEVELOPMENT BANK

Contents

Tables, Figures, and Boxes

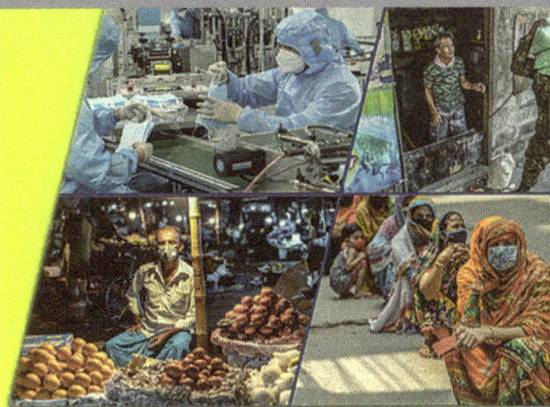

TABLES

FIGURES

BOXES

Foreword

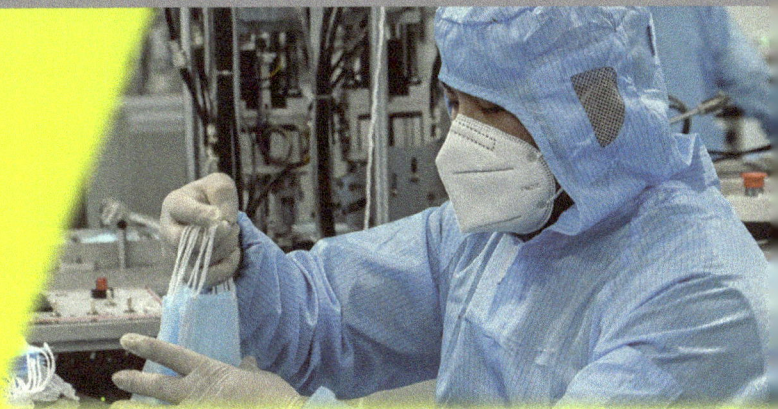

The coronavirus disease (COVID-19) outbreak that began in early 2020 has left tremendous scars on the world economy. The initial supply shock from government-imposed shutdowns at the onset of the pandemic gave rise to an unprecedented demand shock that not only has had health and economic consequences but also social and political ones.

The human toll has been significant, especially if one takes into account the very advanced medical and health systems around the world, particularly in developed countries, which are certainly much better than those in place during the two World Wars and the 1918 flu pandemic. In Asia, the Central and West Asian republics have been most affected when measured by the number of deaths per million population.

The health crisis has been accompanied by an unprecedented economic crisis, with millions of jobs lost and companies closed. To tackle the dual health and economic crises, most governments around the world quickly put in place comprehensive packages that included a wide range of policy measures, mostly in the form of monetary and fiscal actions. These helped the economies cope with the initial supply shock, as factories were shut down, people were asked to stay home, and production and trade collapsed. The objective was to put a floor to the recession and to help unemployed workers and affected firms deal with the shock. Supply chains and sectors such as tourism, transport, and education were badly affected. Shortly afterward, the initial supply shock became a huge demand shock: workers from the worst-hit sectors who were confined at home could not work to earn their wages and hence could not spend.

Most governments have spent significant amounts to manage the crisis and promote recovery. Concurrently, central banks have engineered an unprecedented loosening of their policy stances. Health and income support measures by governments of all Asian Development Bank (ADB) members in the wake of the pandemic are estimated to have reached 12.5% of their gross domestic product as of 18 December 2020. As of this date, the aggregate value of the relief packages that ADB members had announced in response to COVID-19 was approaching $28 trillion. Most of this amount is accounted for by developed countries, with the United States having deployed the largest package at $8 trillion. In the case of ADB's developing members, the top three packages are those of the People's Republic of China, India, and the Republic of Korea, at $2.3 trillion, $412 billion, and $248 billion, respectively. The analysis shows that the actions of governments and central banks in 2020, much more comprehensive than those of the 2008 financial crisis, have been crucial. Without them, the recession would have been even deeper. The large fiscal deficits have helped the private sector maintain a positive financial position.

This report provides an in-depth analysis of how ADB members have dealt with the crisis and the measures they have taken. It also discusses how these measures have been financed, what central banks have done, and how the latter have coordinated their actions with the fiscal arm of the government to support the economy.

Most of the information used in the analysis draws on the ADB COVID-19 Policy Database, which tracks the policy measures and corresponding amounts of funding announced by ADB's 68 members plus several other large economies to combat the COVID-19 pandemic. The analysis is based on data from 20 April to 18 December 2020.

ADB has invested considerable human and intellectual effort in building this database by collecting data, monitoring country situations, and updating it every 2 weeks to provide the latest information. It contains a wealth of knowledge about how members have fought the crisis until now. This database is a public good that attests to ADB's commitment to help Asia. As the pandemic is still evolving during the early months of 2021, with COVID-19 cases increasing significantly in some Asian countries, ADB recognizes that continuous monitoring and analyses like the ones in this report remain critical.

I sincerely hope that the analysis in this report will be useful to policy makers and to the community at large and will help us all better understand the COVID-19 crisis.

Bambang Susantono
Vice-President for Knowledge Management and Sustainable Development

ADB COVID-19 Policy Database

This database provides information on the key economic measures that authorities are taking to combat the COVID-19 pandemic. Measures are classified according to how they work their way through the financial system, and how they affect the financial positions of different sectors of society. The database also tracks non-economic measures.

Read the Background Document

Project Team: Jesus Felipe (Lead), Asian Development Bank; Scott Fullwiler, University of Missouri Kansas City; Gemma Estrada, Asian Development Bank; Maria Susan Torres, Asian Development Bank; Mary Ann Magadia, Asian Development Bank; Donna Faye Bajaro, Asian Development Bank; Maria Hanna Jaber, Asian Development Bank; Remrick Patagan, Asian Development Bank; Marie Ann Cagas, Asian Development Bank; Al-Habbyel Yusoph, University of the Philippines; Simon Alec Askin, University of the Philippines; Martin Alexander Cruz, University of the Philippines; Juan Delgado, Global Economics Group; Héctor Otero, Global Economics Group; and Violeta Rodriguez, Global Economics Group.

Contributors

This report is a project of the Economic Research and Regional Cooperation Department (ERCD) of the Asian Development Bank (ADB). Work on the project started in March 2020, as soon as the World Health Organization declared coronavirus disease (COVID-19) a pandemic. It started with the development of the ADB COVID-19 Policy Database, with the objective of collecting information on the measures ADB members were announcing and implementing to deal with the crisis. The information was meticulously collected and analyzed, and this report is the outcome.

Jesus Felipe, Advisor, ERCD, and Scott Fullwiler, Associate Professor, University of Missouri–Kansas City led the report. Other members of the team include Simon Alec Askin, University of the Philippines; Donna Faye Bajaro, ADB; Marie Anne Cagas, ADB; Martin Alexander Cruz, University of the Philippines; Gemma Estrada, ADB; Maria Hanna Jaber, ADB; Mary Ann Magadia, ADB; Maria Susan Torres, ADB; and Al-Habbyel Yusoph, University of the Philippines.

Maria Hanna Jaber, Maria Susan Torres, and Vanessa Sumo-Van Zandweghe edited the report. Jonathan Yamongan and Judy Yñiguez executed the cover design and editorial layout.

Chapter I

Introduction: COVID-19 and Its Impact

As a result of the coronavirus disease (COVID-19) outbreak that began in early 2020, global growth in 2020 fell by more than 5% (about 5% in Germany, 4.8% in Japan, and 3.5% in the United States [US]), the sharpest decline since World War II. The only major world economy that registered positive growth in 2020 was the People's Republic of China (PRC), which grew at slightly more than 2%. Moreover, goods export growth in dollar terms was positive in only three Asian economies: the PRC; Taipei,China; and Viet Nam (Table 1).

Table 1. Gross Domestic Product and Export Growth Rates, 2020

Economy	Export Growth (%)	Real GDP Growth (%)
Germany	−9.27	−4.96[a]
Indonesia	−2.61	−2.07
Japan	−11.08	−4.79
People's Republic of China	4.03	2.30
Philippines	−10.10	−9.51
Taipei,China	0.21	2.98
Thailand	−5.90	−6.09
United Kingdom	−14.59	−11.3[b]
United States	−12.87	−3.50
Viet Nam	6.52	2.91

GDP = gross domestic product, Q = quarter.

[a] Real GDP growth for Germany was taken from Haver Analytics (accessed 22 February 2021).
[b] As of 22 February 2021, data on the United Kingdom's annual GDP growth had not been released. This figure is the average growth from Q1 to Q3 2020.

Source: CEIC (accessed 19 February 2021).

The combined supply and demand shocks have had unprecedented health and economic consequences. Even before the pandemic, there were fears that another economic crisis was looming. Yet COVID-19 is so different from what anybody could have expected—an economic crisis triggered by a health crisis—that the world did not know how to react to it. Questionable coordination among major economies made the problem worse.

The human toll has been significant. As of early 2021, the number of world deaths due to COVID-19 has surpassed 2 million, and it is increasing at a pace that does not appear to decline: while it took about 7 months for COVID-19 to cause 1 million deaths, it has taken just an additional 3 months for the death toll to reach 2 million. Moreover, while the daily death rate was about 5,000 during the summer of 2020, it has increased to about 13,000. Deaths due to COVID-19 are also affecting more countries. Most of the deaths (as of mid-January 2021) are in Europe and North America at 638,000 and 590,000, respectively, followed by 379,000 in South America; 359,000 in Asia; 81,000 in Africa; and 1,000 in the Pacific islands. The four countries with the largest number of deaths are the US (about 406,000 deaths); Brazil (212,000); India (152,000); and Mexico (144,000) (Table 2). These are large countries with large populations. Midsize countries such as the United Kingdom (UK) (about 94,000 deaths); Italy (83,000); France (69,000); and Spain (58,000) are also among the most affected, and these countries are ranked among the top 10 in per capita terms.[1] Belgium, with almost 1,800 deaths per million tops the world ranking. It is followed by the UK, Italy, the Czech Republic, the US, Spain, and Peru.

Table 2. Number of Deaths and Deaths per Million Population, as of 21 January 2021

Rank	Economy	Deaths per Million Population	Total Number of Deaths
1	Belgium	1,788	20,538
2	United Kingdom	1,405	93,934
3	Italy	1,378	83,083
4	Czech Republic	1,322	14,102
5	United States	1,236	405,800
6	Spain	1,232	57,994
7	Peru	1,198	38,940
8	Mexico	1,128	143,942
9	France	1,036	69,470
10	Argentina	1,022	45,930

Notes: The table refers to countries with populations over 10 million. Ranking is based on deaths per million population.
Source: Asian Development Bank. ADB COVID-19 Policy Database. https://covid19policy.adb.org.

---

[1]   It is important to note that countries have different statistical criteria to count deaths.

In Asia (Table 3), the Central and West Asian republics have been most affected when measured by the number of deaths per million population.

Table 3. Number of Deaths and Deaths per Million Population in Asia, as of 21 January 2021

Rank	Economy	Deaths per Million Population	Total Number of Deaths
1	Armenia	1,014	2,999
2	Georgia	796	2,963
3	Azerbaijan	297	2,972
4	Kyrgyz Republic	284	1,833
5	Kazakhstan	141	2,605
6	India	112	152,377
7	Indonesia	99	26,815
8	Maldives	94	50
9	Philippines	93	10,055
10	Nepal	68	1,953
Other Economies			
1	Islamic Republic of Iran	685	56,767
2	Israel	464	4,204
3	Jordan	409	4,133
4	Iraq	329	12,944
5	Lebanon	309	2,120

Note: Ranking is based on deaths per million population.
Source: Asian Development Bank. ADB COVID-19 Policy Database. https://covid19policy.adb.org.

The speed with which the second million deaths has been reached reminds humanity that this is a race. 2021 arrived with the hope that a vaccine would be available very soon. Although the vaccine brings optimism, the immediate reality is that immunity is still far away. According to the World Health Organization, COVID-19 is today the sixth most important cause of death in the world, at a similar level as lung cancer and ahead of Alzheimer's, diarrhea, diabetes, and kidney diseases. The difference is that COVID-19 did not exist 1 year ago.

The economic crisis that has followed the health crisis has affected millions of jobs and companies. Most countries around the world quickly put in place relief packages. In the case of governments, the pandemic has increased pressure on the state to provide adequate health care and tackle deeper-seated problems such as income inequality. In the case of central banks, the huge rise in the public debt over the past year means a period of ultra-low interest rates will be required to keep the public debt service burdens from rising relative to gross domestic product (GDP).

The Asian Development Bank (ADB) has been tracking the value of the relief packages announced by its members since the start of the pandemic. As of early 2021, this amounted to about $28 trillion. Most of it is accounted for by developed countries (the packages of the PRC and India, both developing countries, are the only ones in the top 10 of largest packages), in the form of both fiscal and monetary measures.

This report's assessment of the situation as of early 2021 is that most governments and central banks across the world seem to have reached a state of "intellectual fatigue" in that the usefulness of the measures implemented so far has been exhausted. Both the governments and central banks are finding it very difficult to come up with new and different measures, amid fears that yet larger fiscal packages would imply larger fiscal deficits. The fate of the recovery at this stage is in the hands of the vaccination process. While the fight against the global financial crisis (GFC) of 2008 was led by central banks (quantitative easing [QE]), this time the role of fiscal policy has been very important, with governments (especially those of the advanced economies) running extremely large deficits (Table 4). Without massive government intervention, this crisis would have been much worse.

Table 4. Fiscal Deficits, 2020

Economy	Consolidated Fiscal Balance (% of GDP)
Australia	−11.47[a]
Canada	−9.68[a]
France	−6.45[a]
Germany	−4.19
India	−5.99
Indonesia	−6.20
Italy	−6.51[a]
Japan	−5.80
New Zealand	−0.62[a]
People's Republic of China	−6.45
Philippines	−7.63
Republic of Korea	−3.44[a]
Singapore	−6.75
Spain	−8.12[a]
Thailand	1.00
United Kingdom	−12.90[a]
United States	−15.98

GDP = gross domestic product, Q = quarter.
[a] Annualized data as of Q3 2020.
Source: CEIC (accessed 2 March 2021).

The study estimates that health and income support measures by governments in the wake of the pandemic have reached 10.4% of global GDP as of 18 December 2020. This compares to a fiscal support of 2% of world GDP during the GFC, which is already a substantial amount. Across Asia, the range of commitments for health and income support measures in response to the downturn has been varied. Japan and Singapore committed around 44% and 14% of their respective GDPs to support measures in 2020 (although at least half of Japan's commitment could be classified as quasi-monetary). In poorer countries, health and income support injections ranged between 0.04% and 5% of GDP. Thailand was an exception, where the government committed 8.2% of 2019 GDP to spending programs, most of which remain stalled. Just how much of these commitments will be disbursed is open to question.

The important point is that the idea of austerity has sharply reversed from the policy response to the previous crisis only 12 years ago. Fiscal demand management was already gaining popularity, but the pandemic has thrown remaining budgetary caution to the wind—governments have spent vast sums to manage the current crisis and promote recovery. They have learned over the past decade that interest payment on debt can be kept down by central bank asset purchases, while central banks have learned how to conduct monetary policy in an environment with large amounts of excess reserves that, contrary to long-held views, has not proven to be inflationary. There are now fewer perceived limits to state borrowing than there were 10 years ago.

Concurrently, central banks have engineered an unprecedented loosening of their policy stances. Financing of government deficits by the US Federal Reserve, Bank of Canada, Bank of Japan, and Bank of England has amounted to $3.5 trillion over the past year—equivalent to 3.87% of global GDP. Across Asia, the largest rate cuts have been those in the Philippines and Viet Nam. The combination of monetary expansion alongside fiscal expansion has meant that, unlike in previous rounds of QE, the stimulus packages have found their way into the real economy instead of getting stuck in the financial system.

The extent to which economic damage has been averted by these measures will probably never be known. Governments will claim economic successes and blame COVID-19 for failures. The data will be unable to differentiate. Policy measures have been highly varied, with many governments perceiving the problem to be a conventional aggregate demand shortfall. In reality, the government-imposed lockdowns were a severe shock to supply chains. In that respect, government efforts to support businesses and households in maintaining their pre-pandemic financial positions during the lockdowns in what they hoped would be temporary layoffs were by far the best targets for macroeconomic policy responses to the pandemic.

The initial months of massive government support were followed by questions about how to move on to the recovery phase. The problem is that the pandemic has not disappeared, thus delaying the recovery. Lockdowns are still in effect or have been reintroduced in many places, while in other cases, new waves of infections and deaths have emerged. Hence, it has been very difficult to design a rebound strategy. The first vaccines were finally introduced in advanced economies in December 2020. Results are yet to be seen, although the mood has changed and there is a sense of tentative optimism. Most developing countries are significantly behind.

Even before the pandemic, the failure to adequately reform policy frameworks after the 2008 GFC arguably led to stagnation in many economies in the last decade. That the COVID-19 recession is undoubtedly of a far greater scale than the GFC suggests the need for bolder monetary, supply-side, and industrial policy measures than in the post-GFC period, which is perhaps finally clear. These measures are needed to catalyze and sustain economic relief, recovery, and restructuring, in order to address economic maladies prior to the pandemic and the post-lockdown malaise.

The COVID-19 crisis presents the world with an opportunity to do better moving forward. There is much to learn and do in order to progress, including abandoning the very modes of thinking—for example, that all fiscal deficits are intrinsically bad—which have led to the confusion and disarray the world economy is in.

This report is a unique source of information to understand how ADB members have dealt with the COVID-19 crisis. It offers a distinct taxonomy of measures based on their effects on the financial statements of the government and the private sector. It also offers a statistical analysis of the size of the packages and a discussion of fiscal deficits and monetization applied to the COVID-19 response in Asia. Finally, it provides an analysis of the impacts of COVID-19 and the countries' macroeconomic policy responses on the financial positions of their private sectors.

Most of the information used in this report draws on the ADB COVID-19 Policy Database, which can be accessed at https://covid19policy.adb.org. The analysis is based on data until 18 December 2020. The report is structured as follows. Chapter II explains the criteria used to arrange the information in the database. Chapter III provides a descriptive summary of the specific measures ADB members implemented in 2020 and the amounts announced by the governments. Chapter IV provides a comparison of the packages implemented by several ADB members. Chapter V is a statistical analysis of the packages and how they correlate with variables such as the number of people infected with COVID-19. Chapter VI offers a discussion of how central banks and treasuries have coordinated their operations within the context of unprecedented central bank support of government during the pandemic.

Finally, Chapter VII provides an analysis of the status of the sectoral balances as of late 2020. This chapter's goal is to understand whether the policy responses to the pandemic were sufficient in maintaining, supporting, and/or restoring private sector financial positions. By construction, the financial balances of the private sector, government, and foreign sector (capital account) add up to zero. Hence, a fiscal deficit has a counterpart in the national accounts, namely the surplus of the private sector (the fiscal and monetary expansions are stored as savings and this shows up as an increase in household and corporate deposits). It is also important to analyze which part of the private sector—households, nonfinancial firms, or the financial sector—has seen an increase in its surplus. For this analysis, the report uses data collected from flow-of-funds accounts.

As the objective of the report is to take stock of what happened during 2020, specific recommendations on what to do to move forward are beyond its scope. Nevertheless, a few important insights have come out of the analysis, especially with regard to the large fiscal deficits incurred by ADB members during 2020 and potentially beyond.

First, whether the ADB members' fiscal deficits are large enough is not the right question, since deficits can be large in cases where policy responses are large or small (the latter case could be due to automatic stabilizers' effects on budget positions in a deep recession). The relevant question is, instead, whether policy measures maintained, supported, and/or restored private sector financial positions, and the policy insight is to recognize that there are options ranging from very large to essentially negligible effects on the government's fiscal balance or the national debt.

Second, the large fiscal deficits in many countries have led to questions about debt sustainability. Indeed, some commentators have warned against deficit financing. Instead of recognizing the need for consistently countercyclical fiscal policies over the duration of business cycles, they insist on minimal annual budget shortfalls in the short term and on balancing budgets by 2021, regardless of the recession's nature and duration. Yet government and central bank (as currency issuers) finances do not operate like those of a family with a budget constraint. Indeed, a government deficit creates income for the recipients; and bond sales neither reduce this income nor return it to the government. Given how modern central banks conduct their monetary policies by setting and managing the short-term interest rate, the old textbook-style notions of monetization do not, in fact, happen. Bond sales are monetary operations to achieve a central bank's interest rate target; the alternative is interest on reserves or a zero interest rate policy. There is no "helicopter money" alternative to these in real-world central bank operations. Central banks supply at least enough reserve balances to settle government bond auctions and necessarily drive interest rates on government debt in domestic currency regardless of who owns it. In short, monetization is not the horror economists for generations have assumed it to be, but it is also benign to the degree that it cannot be a solution in itself.

Third, a related issue is the fear of inflation by those who claim that more government spending will cause a price spiral. The reality is that most packages that countries announced in 2020 ought to be labeled relief packages rather than stimulus packages. Perhaps 2021 packages will be more of the second type, especially as the health crisis recedes and economic activity resumes. As noted above, the COVID crisis hit the supply side of the economy first, as people could not go to work and businesses closed, leading to falling production and incomes. The purpose of the first rounds of government spending in 2020 was to keep the economy on life support by providing relief. Even as rising vaccination rates will help get people back to work, households, firms, and state or local governments will continue to bear the burden of nearly a year's worth of unpaid bills, depressed income and revenues, and extra burdens imposed by the pandemic. Packages in 2021 will go a long way toward providing relief, including the Biden administration's latest round of stimulus checks announced in March 2021, which will go to most families to help cover basic bills. The propensity to consume out of these checks will not be high, however, as most people will use them to pay down debts or replenish savings. With production rebounding, even if the checks are used for consumption, they will hardly cause inflation.

Finally, the size of the packages per capita is mostly explained by countries' GDP per capita. Richer countries have announced very large packages. This variable alone explains most of the variation in package per capita, much more than the number of COVID-19 cases or deaths. This has obvious implications for future policy debates at the national and international levels. In particular, the international financial and policy institutions might want to consider whether national responses effectively set by per capita GDPs are consistent with how countries should respond to future financial crises and pandemics. If, on the other hand, citizens of poorer nations would be significantly better off spending far more than what their per capita GDP suggests they will or can, then the time to design and institutionalize such capabilities is already here. The ability of so many countries to incur large deficits, maintain low interest rates, and avoid sustained exchange rate depreciations as they responded to COVID-19 suggests that aligning policy responses to the public's needs, whether in line with per capita GDP or not, is more possible than thought prior to COVID-19.

Chapter II

The ADB COVID-19 Policy Database

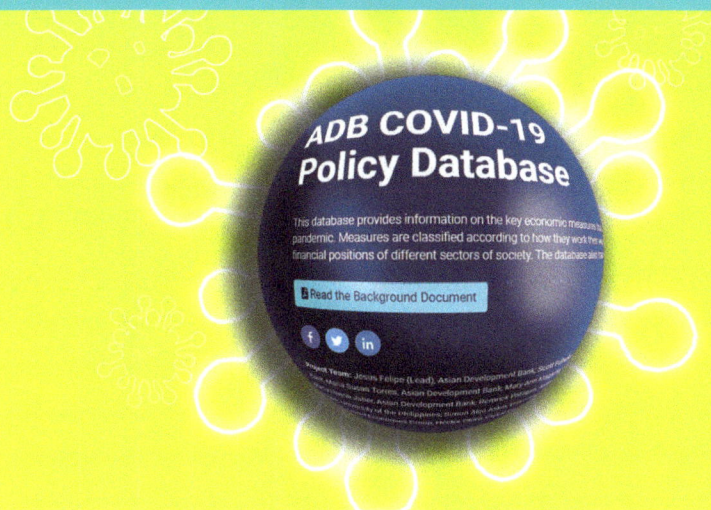

This chapter introduces the ADB COVID-19 Policy Database. This database contains detailed information on the measures that all ADB members have taken to combat COVID-19. The primary information comes from both national sources and data collected by international organizations. Most of the analysis in this report draws on the information and figures contained in this database. This chapter explains the key concepts that underlie the taxonomy used to construct the database, which comes from information collected on the key economic measures that authorities announced in 2020 to combat the COVID-19 pandemic.[2]

The database covers the 68 members of ADB; the European Central Bank (ECB); the European Union (EU); and nine other economies in Africa, Latin America, and Europe (Table 5).[3] They represent 92.4% of global GDP and 79.9% of the world's population.

The rest of the chapter is structured as follows. Section II.A explains each policy measure based on differences in operational details and/or financial statement effects. These measures are not based on the standard conceptions of fiscal and monetary policies but instead capture the financial positions that central banks and governments have taken relative to the private sector and state or local governments. Section II.B discusses how these measures are financed, whether through the central bank, the government, or other financing mechanisms. Finally, section II.C provides an overview on how the total COVID-19 response package is computed for each economy and how measures are aggregated across economies.

---

[2]   Felipe and Fullwiler (2020a) provide a detailed guide on the ADB COVID-19 Policy Database. The database can be accessed at https://covid19policy.adb.org. The complete list of measures is listed in the Appendix.

[3]   Data are available on a biweekly basis from 20 April to 18 December 2020.

Table 5. List of Economies in the ADB COVID-19 Policy Database

CENTRAL AND WEST ASIA
Afghanistan
Armenia
Azerbaijan
Georgia
Kazakhstan
Kyrgyz Republic
Pakistan
Tajikistan
Turkmenistan
Uzbekistan

EAST ASIA
Hong Kong, China
Mongolia
People's Republic of China
Republic of Korea
Taipei,China

PACIFIC
Cook Islands
Federated States of Micronesia
Fiji
Kiribati
Marshall Islands
Nauru
Niue
Palau
Papua New Guinea
Samoa
Solomon Islands
Tonga
Tuvalu
Vanuatu

SOUTH ASIA
Bangladesh
Bhutan
India
Maldives
Nepal
Sri Lanka

SOUTHEAST ASIA
Brunei Darussalam
Cambodia
Indonesia
Lao People's Democratic Republic
Malaysia
Myanmar
Philippines
Singapore
Thailand
Timor-Leste
Viet Nam

OTHER ECONOMIES
Arab Republic of Egypt
Argentina
Brazil
Islamic Republic of Iran
Mexico
Nigeria
Russian Federation
Saudi Arabia
South Africa

OTHER ADB MEMBERS
Australia
Austria
Belgium
Canada
Denmark
Finland
France
Germany
Ireland
Italy
Japan
Luxembourg
Netherlands
New Zealand
Norway
Portugal
Spain
Sweden
Switzerland
Turkey
United Kingdom
United States

EUROPEAN INSTITUTIONS
European Central Bank
European Union

ADB = Asian Development Bank, COVID-19 = coronavirus disease.
Source: Asian Development Bank. ADB COVID-19 Policy Database. https://covid19policy.adb.org.

A.   Categorization of Policy Measures

To understand the different policy actions in response to COVID-19, the policy database categorizes these actions according to their differences in operational details and/or financial statement effects (Table 6). Operational details define the path a given measure takes to affect the financial system, spending, production, and so forth. These policy responses fall into the following categories:

(i)   provide liquidity to financial and nonfinancial businesses and/or state, local, or regional governments;

(ii)   encourage credit creation by the financial sector; and

(iii)   directly fund households, businesses, and/or state, local, or regional governments.

Financial statement effects of a given measure answer one of the following questions:

(i)   Who, if anyone, bears the financial burden of the measure and in what form?

(ii)   Does the measure create more debt or more income (e.g., net worth or equity, other things being equal) for the recipients?

Table 6. Categorization of Measures according to Operational Details and Financial Statement Effects

Operational Details	Financial Statement Effects
Provide liquidity	**Measure 01** ■ Loans from the central bank or government to the private sector and state, local, or regional governments ■ Government or central bank purchases of short-term assets from the private sector ■ Regulatory or other changes that do not directly alter private sector financial statements
Encourage credit creation	**Measure 02** ■ Increases in liabilities of the private sector and state, local, or regional governments to the national government or central bank through long-term loans to the financial sector (to enable further lending to the financial and nonfinancial sectors) or secondary market purchases of securities issued by the financial sector; businesses; or state, local, or regional governments ■ Interest rate changes, loan guarantees, regulatory changes to encourage private credit creation, and other policies to support long-term lending
Directly fund	**Measure 03** ■ Increases in recipients' liabilities through long-term direct loans from the government or central bank **Measure 04** ■ Increases in ownership claims of the government or central bank through equity investments in the business and/or financial sectors **Measure 05** ■ Increases in income or reductions in costs or obligations through government transfer payments, loan cancellations, tax cuts, payment deferrals, and so forth

Source: Felipe, Jesus, and Scott Fullwiler. 2020. "ADB COVID-19 Policy Database: A Guide." *Asian Development Review* 37 (2): 1–20.

In Table 6, the left column repeats the three categories of operational details. The respective potential financial statement outcomes of a given measure are to the right of the corresponding operational detail categories. In order to provide liquidity, for instance, governments or central banks can (i) lend (expanding the borrowers' liabilities in order to obtain central bank liabilities) via existing or expanded standing facilities; (ii) purchase financial assets (exchanging the sellers' financial assets for central bank liabilities); or (iii) undertake actions which do not directly alter private sector financial statements in the sense that there are no accompanying transactions (though they may encourage or enable financial institutions' subsequent actions and thereby lead to changes in their financial statements indirectly), such as relaxing regulations (e.g., lowering required minimum liquidity ratios), expanding the range of acceptable collateral for secured loans from the central bank, and so on.

The framework in Table 6 shows five measures in the taxonomy of the ADB COVID-19 Policy Database. Measures 01–04 mostly correspond to central bank actions, while Measure 05 corresponds to government initiatives. Three additional measures are effectively double counting from an accounting perspective but are nonetheless important measures. These are labeled Measures 06–08 in the Appendix. These three measures are sources of funds, while Measures 01–05 are uses of funds. Measure 08 corresponds to international assistance received by an economy, whereas Measure 09 corresponds to international assistance from the point of view of the donor economy. Measure 10 is added to take into account actions for which the current information is unclear about the particular measure where they should be added. A brief discussion of each measure follows.

Measure 01 (liquidity support) has three subcategories. Measure 01A refers to short-term lending to the private sector and state, local, or regional governments; and purchase of short-term financial assets to provide liquidity. Measure 01B refers to support policies for short-term lending, which include adjustments in collateral requirements for borrowing from the central bank or government, payments system policies, reserve requirements, and other liquidity regulations (such as the liquidity coverage ratio, and so forth).[4] Measure 01C includes foreign exchange operations or domestic lending in foreign currency (including domestic foreign currency swap markets) to support domestic liquidity in foreign currency.

Measure 02 (credit creation) also has three subcategories. Measure 02A is for financial sector lending and funding, which include secondary market purchases of mortgage-backed securities, corporate bonds, collateralized loan obligations, or bond exchange-traded funds, and loans to the financial sector. Measure 02B includes support policies for long-term lending and is further categorized into 02B1 for interest rate adjustments and 02B2 for other policies to support long-term lending such as regulatory adjustments to (usually) relax capital requirements, bank oversight, and lending standards.[5] Measure 02C is for loan guarantees.

Measure 03 has two subcategories. Measure 03A covers long-term (greater than 1 year) direct lending to businesses and households and to state, local, or regional governments. Measure 03B covers forbearances.

Measure 04—equity investments by the government or central bank—currently has no subcategories.

Measure 05 has three subcategories for health and income support: those directly related to health care and public health (Measure 05A), all other income support (Measure 05B), and announced measures that cannot be disaggregated between 05A and 05B (Measure 05C). Measure 05B is further disaggregated into six subcategories: 05B1 covers all deferrals of tax and social security contributions; 05B2 covers nonpayment or reduction of taxes and contributions, which may be temporary or permanent, for example, tax holidays and tax credits or subsidies; 05B3 covers direct payments in cash or in kind, deferrals on rent and utility payments, and measures that directly provide jobs (public or private); 05B4 covers all subsidies to businesses, including covering workers'

---

[4]   Measure 01B also covers regulations to limit distribution of dividends by banks if this constrains their capacity to meet their clients' liquidity needs.

[5]   Similar to Measure 01B, Measure 02B usually does not have an amount. However, if there is an estimated amount of the impact of a particular measure under 01B or 02B (e.g., a reduction in the reserve ratio), then the amount is reported as part of an economy's total package.

wages (usually partial) so employers can continue to provide jobs or retain their current employees; 05B5 covers funding for cultural activities, libraries, infrastructure, or environment-related spending with multiplier effects, and also subsidies for training or reskilling and other measures that indirectly create jobs; 05B6 covers income support measures that fit the description of Measure 05B but information provided by primary sources is not sufficient to determine where the measure fits among the five subcategories.

These measures and subcategories do not easily fit the standard conceptions of monetary and fiscal policies. Measures 01–03 relate mostly to loans, financial regulations, interest rate changes, and so forth, which are most often associated with monetary policy.[6] Measure 05 directly impacts the government sector's budget position, which is commonly associated with fiscal policy.[7] The standard classification of policies into fiscal and monetary misses a lot of important things. This is because if the distinction between fiscal and monetary policy is simply whether the government or central bank implemented a measure, then it is not a useful distinction—saying "monetary" or "fiscal" is redundant with saying "the central bank did it" or "the government did it." In that case, what matters is who did something, not what was done. In the case of the ADB COVID-19 Policy Database, it is the opposite—what matters is not who did it but what was done. Both government and central bank can make loans for working capital or for the long term; they can both invest in private sector equity; they can both change regulatory requirements, etc. Therefore, what matters is what they did, or how private financial positions were affected, and what the governments and central banks have actually taken onto their financial statements. Because the approach here separates the actions by effects on financial statements and differences in operations, if the government provides a loan guarantee, for instance, then this is a contingent liability that does not affect the government's financial statements (i.e., it does not affect the government's budget position) unless the borrower of the guaranteed loan defaults.[8] In the list of measures, the loan guarantee fits Measure 02C, while a default on a loan with a guarantee subtracts from Measure 02C and adds the same amount to Measure 05B.[9] Consequently, while Measure 05 is the closest among the measures to a typical definition of fiscal policy, the value of Measure 05 will not necessarily equal what a nation may announce as a fiscal package.[10]

To better distinguish among Measures 01–04, Table 7 shows the typical differences in maturities, markets, lenders, and borrowers. Although these characteristics are typical, they are not necessarily universal or present in every circumstance.

---

[6]   In the case of Measures 01B and 02B, actions that encourage lending to the private sector do not have the same effect on private financial positions as actions that create private income. Traditional views of fiscal and monetary policies, however, usually just consider whether aggregate demand increased, not the financial positions.

[7]   Both governments and central banks engage in financial regulation, which mostly appears in Measure 01B and Measure 02B.

[8]   If the central bank makes a loan that defaults, it comes out of the government budget as if the government had made the loan or guaranteed the loan. Effectively, both would be in Measure 05 (once the default occurs), but mainstream view refers to one measure as fiscal and to the other as monetary.

[9]   Loan defaults by households that are covered by guarantees are included in Measure 05B3, while those of businesses are recorded in 05B4.

[10]   A good example of this is the US Coronavirus Aid, Relief, and Economic Security (CARES) Act, which has a total value of $2.2 trillion but includes about $775 billion in guarantees (Measure 02C) to banks in the Paycheck Protection Program and to the Federal Reserve, as well as smaller allocations for loans to private businesses (Measures 01A and 03A).

Table 7. Summary of (Typical) Differences among Measures 01–04

Feature	Liquidity Support (01)	Credit Creation (02)	Long-Term Direct Lending (03)	Equity Support (04)
Maturities	≤1 year	>1 year	>1 year	–
Markets	Any short-term credit market	Secondary debt markets or loan purchases	Primary debt markets, direct loans	Equities (primary and/or secondary, ETFs, etc.)
Borrowers	Financial institutions; nonfinancial businesses; state, regional, local governments; central banks and official accounts (currency swaps and similar arrangements)	Financial institutions (who then lend to the private sector)	Nonfinancial businesses; state, regional, local governments; households	–
Lenders	Central bank and government	Central bank and government	Central bank and government	Central bank and government

– = not applicable, ETFs = exchange-traded funds.
Source: Felipe, Jesus, and Scott Fullwiler. 2020. "ADB COVID-19 Policy Database: A Guide." *Asian Development Review* 37 (2): 1–20.

The database contains five additional measures. Three of these measures are consistent with Table 6 but effectively double count from an accounting perspective. They are (i) Measure 06: redirecting or reallocating previously budgeted spending, (ii) Measure 07: central bank financing government in primary or secondary markets, and (iii) Measure 08: international assistance (borrower or recipient).

Measure 06 is double counting because it is previously budgeted spending (already allocated or budgeted) that is redirected or reallocated and has been previously accounted for in government budget position projections. Therefore, in theory, entries under this measure should not affect subsequent projections to the budget position.

Measure 07 is double counting because central bank purchases of government securities or direct loans to the government double count government deficits (except to the degree that the purchases or loans become greater than COVID-19-related deficits), which are already included in Measures 01–05 (mostly Measure 05, though government may be engaged in Measures 01–04).[11] Measure 07 contains two subcategories: (i) direct lending and government reserve drawdown (Measure 07A), and (ii) secondary market purchase of government securities (Measure 07B). Central bank's purchases of government securities or direct loans to government are not adding to the stimulus or the government's deficit, at least not quantitatively. It might reduce interest rates on government debt and encourage lending (Measure 02B1), but it is double counting the deficit if it adds to private incomes. With the central bank's financial support of government, there is always controversy about the potential for inflation and/or the threat of fiscal dominance. Less often understood is that governments and their central

---

[11]   While central bank lending to the government may be considered as providing liquidity, it is not recorded in either Measure 01 (liquidity support) or Measure 02 (credit creation) but is part of Measure 07, which is not added to an economy's total package. Thus, there is no double counting.

banks are already carrying out operations daily that are inherently interdependent. Whereas standard thinking has been that central bank support of government deficits amounts to "printing money" and/or "monetizing government debt," actual operations and accounting show this not to be the case. This will be discussed in detail in chapter VI. Instead, these operations simply replace an interest-earning government liability with an interest-earning central bank liability, though they obviously also can enable more central bank influence over risk-free interest rates in the domestic currency.

Measure 08, international assistance received, is also double counting because it is receiving funds, not spending, lending, or investing them. It contains two subcategories: (i) swaps and clearing arrangements from the borrower economy's side (Measure 08A), and (ii) international loans and grants received (Measure 08B) from ADB (Measure 08B1) and other institutions (Measure 08B2).

Two more policy measures complete the list. Measure 09 is international assistance given by a lender or donor. This is the mirror image of Measure 08, from the point of view of the donor economy.[12] It contains two subcategories: (i) swaps and clearing arrangements provided as lender (Measure 09A), and (ii) international loans and grants given (Measure 09B). It is not double counting from the perspective of the individual nation. Finally, Measure 10 is a black box used to keep track of a nation's actions or announced measures that fit somewhere within Measures 01–05, but press releases and other primary sources do not yet provide sufficient information to determine the exact nature of the measure or amount. Details on actual measures will be discussed in Chapter III.

It is important to note that the macroeconomic impact of each measure can be classified depending on its purpose and effect. First, every measure's operational details for the main macroeconomic Measures 01–05 are consistent with either stimulus (i.e., results in multiplier effects greater than 0) or prevention of further macroeconomic decline (i.e., similar to automatic stabilizers but discretionary in this case).[13] Whether Measures 06 and 07 can be classified as a stimulus or prevention depends on the context. Measures 08 and 09 are prevention measures.

Second, the measures could have one or several of the following effects: (i) change or support to asset prices, (ii) private debt creation, (iii) delay in payment obligations, (iv) government or central bank claims on private sector, (v) contingent liabilities of government or central bank, (vi) direct increase in private sector net financial assets, and (vii) double counting. Measures 01–05 involve some combination of asset price changes or support and/or financial position effects for the private sector; Measures 06, 07, and 08 are double counting; and asset price changes or support is possible for Measures 07 and 08. The effect of Measure 09 depends on the recipient economy. These effects are all consistent across economies implementing the same measure.[14]

---

[12]   Measure 09 of all lender or donor economies is excluded in the computation of the total package across economies. However, this measure is included in the calculation of the individual economy packages. In the case of the EU, funding to its member states is recorded in Measure 09B. The programs or packages funded by the EU can be considered as part of Measures 01–05 of each member state, hence these are recorded in the latter's total package.

[13]   To illustrate, note in Table 6 that the classification of Measure 01 in terms of operational details is to provide liquidity. Such liquidity provision in a financial crisis like the current one is operationally not a stimulus. These operations are aimed at preventing a still worse crisis, or, so to speak, putting a floor underneath it.

[14]   Felipe and Fullwiler (2020a) provide a sample worksheet showing the macroeconomic impacts of each measure.

B.   Financing of COVID-19 Measures

As noted earlier, there is a use and funding relationship between Measures 01–05 (and Measure 10, discussed below) and Measures 06–08, respectively (which is the accounting corollary of the just explained "double counting" for these measures). From the point of view of the uses, Measures 01–04 are mostly funded by the central bank (self-financed) and partly by the government. Measure 05 is funded by the government's bond sales to the nongovernment sector (which may be purchased in the secondary market by the central bank in Measure 07B), central bank loans or primary market purchases of government bonds (Measure 07A), drawdown of existing reserves (Measure 07A), and partly by international assistance (Measure 08B). From the point of view of the funding sources, Measure 06 is also a source of government spending, lending, or investing, but it is mutually exclusive from Measures 01–05 in this taxonomy since where the spending has been reallocated to is already in Measure 06. As noted, in Measure 07, the central bank directly or indirectly funds the government, which then appears in the latter's actions across Measures 01–05. Measure 08A directly goes to the central bank, providing funding for activities in Measure 01C. Finally, as noted, Measure 08B is a source of funds for the government and likely ends up in Measure 05. These relationships are summarized in Figure 1.

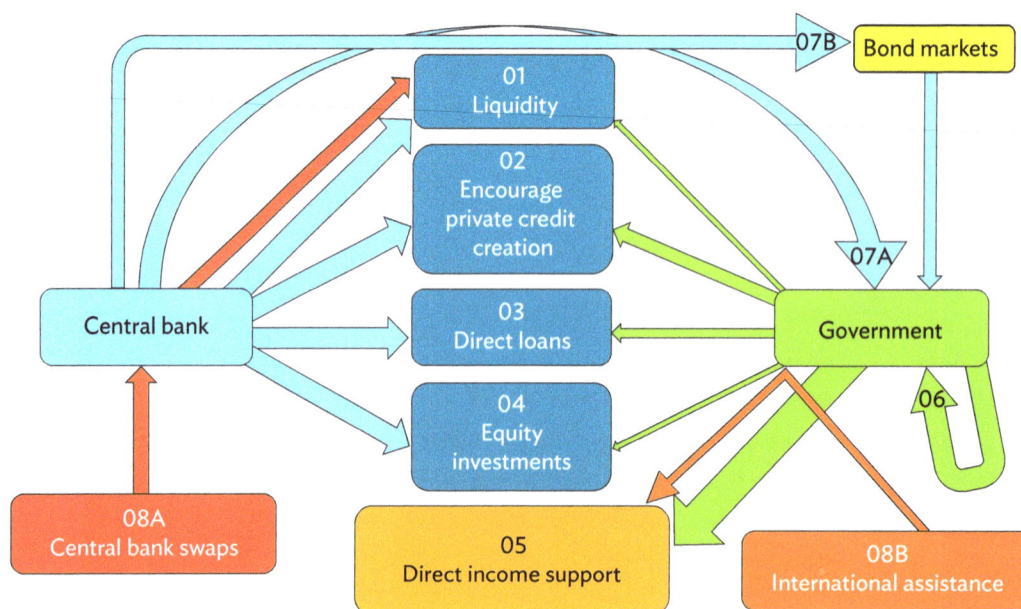

Figure 1. COVID-19 Measures and Their Funding

COVID-19 = coronavirus disease.

Note: The width of the arrows is intended to give an idea of the approximate relative size of the funding. The thicker the arrow the larger the funding.

Source: Felipe, Jesus, and Scott Fullwiler. 2020. "ADB COVID-19 Policy Database: A Guide." *Asian Development Review* 37 (2): 1–20.

C.   Aggregation of Policy Measures

To get an idea of a nation's total COVID-19 policy response, Measures 01–05 and 09 are combined. Together, these measures capture the financial positions the central bank and government have taken relative to the private sector and state or local governments across their cumulative policy responses— lending to the private sector and state or local governments, contingent liabilities, equity investments, foreign exchange intervention, lending in domestic markets in foreign currencies, lending domestic currencies to other central banks, and direct transfers of income.

For aggregation across economies, however, Measures 01–05 are the appropriate ones to add. Measure 09 must be dropped because it double counts both Measure 08 and, more importantly, Measure 01C, in the context of a compilation across economies.

The ADB COVID-19 Policy Database presents individual economy worksheets in its Policy Measures page.[15] Each worksheet provides the sum of the amounts in Measures 01–05 (in US dollars), plus the amount in Measure 10 (No breakdown). For lenders, Measure 09 is added. This is referred to as the total package provided. It should be emphasized that Measures 01–05 (and 10) include aspects as diverse as central bank or government purchases of assets (Measure 01), the expected impact of lower interest rates in terms of credit creation (Measure 02), and actual government spending (Measure 05). The reason for adding them up is that these measures are consistent with either stimulus (i.e., results in multiplier effects greater than 0) or prevention of further macroeconomic decline (i.e., similar to automatic stabilizers but discretionary in this case). They are all "response measures." Further, any monetary sum cannot fully represent the measures taken, given that authorities adjust interest rates, liquidity regulations, and capital regulations. It is also important to recognize that measures (and amounts) announced change very often.

The aggregation of measures does not suggest that these individual measures are qualitatively the same. If they were, there would be no reason to have categories in the first place. Summing across economies for Measures 01–05, and summing Measures 01–05 and 09 together for an individual economy, gives the total financial positions that have been assumed vis-à-vis the private sector and state or local government sectors. A larger sum tells us a response was likely to have been larger, but does not necessarily tell us that the response was better.

Finally, there are significant differences in what economies report and the quality of reporting across economies. Some do not provide figures for measures that could be represented in monetary terms and have only issued policy statements without monetary amounts. Further, significant portions of Measures 01 and 02 do not always lend themselves to such reporting of numerical estimates (such as relaxation of liquidity or capital requirements). While it is useful to calculate a nation's total policy response or to compare responses across economies, it is also important to understand what is included and not included in the calculation.[16]

---

[15]   Individual economy worksheets can be accessed through https://covid19policy.adb.org/policy-measures.
[16]   For these reasons, users of the ADB COVID-19 Policy Database should exercise caution when making comparisons across economies.

D.   Conclusions

In summary, the ADB COVID-19 Policy Database adopts a meaningful way of classifying the economic measures announced by authorities in 2020 to deal with the pandemic. The classification of these measures is based on differences in operational details (whether providing liquidity, encouraging credit creation, or directly providing funding) and/or financial statement effects (who bears the financing, and whether the measure is adding more income or more debt). To the extent possible, the measures' monetary amounts are aggregated to provide an idea of the size of the economies' policy responses. Chapter III discusses these measures in relation to the actual policies and amounts announced by the different economies.

Appendix. List of Policy Measures in the ADB COVID-19 Policy Database

Measure		Detailed Measure Name
01	Liquidity support	Support the normal functioning of money markets and short-term finance
01A	Short-term lending	Lending to the private sector and state, local, or regional governments, and asset purchases to provide liquidity
01B	Support policies for short-term lending	Nonlending actions and regulatory adjustments: collateral requirements, payments system policies, liquidity regulations, reserve requirements, etc.
01C	Forex operations	Foreign exchange operations or domestic lending in foreign currency
02	Credit creation	Encourage private credit creation
02A	Financial sector lending/funding	Secondary market purchases of securities (greater than 1 year to maturity), and loans to the financial sector
02B	Support policies for long-term lending	Interest rate and other regulatory adjustments: capital requirements, credit and lending standards, oversight, etc.
02B1	Interest rate adjustments	–
02B2	Other policies to support long-term lending	–
02C	Loan guarantees	–
03	Direct long-term lending	Long-term direct lending to businesses, households, and state, local, or regional governments, and forbearance
03A	Long-term lending	Long-term direct lending to businesses, households, and state, local, or regional governments
03B	Forbearance	–
04	Equity support	Equity claims on the private sector (equities, primary and/or secondary, ETFs, etc.)
05	Health and income support	–
05A	Health support	–
05B	Income support	–

continued on next page

Appendix *continued*

Measure		Detailed Measure Name
05B1	Tax and contribution deferrals and policy changes	–
05B2	Tax and contribution rates reduction	–
05B3	Subsidies to individuals and households	–
05B4	Subsidies to businesses	–
05B5	Indirect income support	–
05B6	No breakdown (income support)	–
05C	No breakdown (health and income support)	–
06	Budget reallocation	Redirecting or reallocating previously budgeted spending
07	Central bank financing government	–
07A	Direct lending and reserve drawdown	–
07B	Secondary purchase: government securities	–
08	International assistance received	–
08A	Swaps	Swaps and clearing arrangements (borrower)
08B	International loans/grants	–
08B1	Asian Development Bank	–
08B2	Other	–
09	International assistance provided	–
09A	Swaps	Swaps and clearing arrangements (lender)
09B	International loans/grants	–
10	No breakdown	–

– = not applicable, ADB = Asian Development Bank, COVID-19 = coronavirus disease, ETFs = exchange-traded funds.

Source: Asian Development Bank. ADB COVID-19 Policy Database. https://covid19policy.adb.org.

Chapter III

What Did Economies Do to Fight the COVID-19 Pandemic in 2020?

This chapter takes a closer look at the COVID-19 response packages ADB members have implemented—the size of the packages, how they changed over time, amounts by region, and the specific measures taken. Section III.A discusses the total packages (Measures 01–05 and 10) and identifies which economies have allocated the largest amounts in both absolute and relative terms. Section III.B breaks down the total packages into Measures 01–04 and Measure 05, with loan guarantees (Measure 02C) separated as a special category. As noted in Chapter II, the categorization of measures in the ADB COVID-19 Policy Database is not based on the standard conceptions of fiscal and monetary policies but captures the financial positions the central bank and government have taken relative to the private sector and state or local governments. The latter part of section III.B consists of an analysis of each measure (Measures 01–05 and Measures 09–10), for both ADB's developing members and other ADB members. The remarks for each measure consist of, whenever applicable, (i) a short description of the measure and its corresponding submeasures; (ii) economies that have allocated large amounts to that measure; (iii) trends over time; and (iv) specific actions that economies have implemented under that measure. The latter part of the section provides details on the stimulus package announced in the US in December 2020. Lastly, section III.C discusses the measures that are not added to the total package because of double counting, which was explained in Chapter II (Measures 06–08).

A.   How Large Are the Total Packages?

Table 8 shows the total COVID-19 response package as of 20 April, 15 June, 21 September, and 18 December 2020. The table is divided into ADB's developing members and other ADB members, with the former further split by region. It is important to note that significant portions of these announced packages are intentions, and that only in due time will we know the true amounts of the packages compared to what was initially authorized.

As of 18 December 2020, the total package of the 68 members of ADB (including the ECB and the EU) amounted to $27.4 trillion, up from $15.6 trillion as of 20 April 2020, or an increase of 75.6%. ADB's developing members contributed $3.6 trillion (an increase of 97% over the April figure). ADB's other members contributed $17.5 trillion, while the ECB and the EU added another $6.3 trillion.

Out of the 68 ADB members, Niue is the only country that has not publicly announced any specific monetary amount to combat COVID-19. Fifty members have packages of at most $100 billion each; 62 members have at most $800 billion each; and five member economies have at least $1.7 trillion each. The US has the largest package at $8.1 trillion, and the PRC is the only ADB developing member in the top five.

Of the $11.8 trillion increase in the total package between 20 April and 18 December 2020, $9.9 trillion came from ADB's developing members and other ADB members, while the ECB and the EU contributed the remaining $1.9 trillion. Looking across ADB's developing members, East Asia contributed 75.5% of the region's total package as of 18 December 2020, followed by South Asia with 11.8% of the total. These two regions also had the largest percentage increases between 20 April and 18 December 2020 at 88% and 488.6%, respectively.

Data across the four dates in Table 8 show that total packages had started stabilizing as early as 21 September 2020. ADB's developing members and other ADB members registered 97.2% and 82.5% of the total increase in their packages, respectively, as of this date.

Table 8. COVID-19 Response Packages, as of 20 April, 15 June, 21 September, and 18 December 2020
($ million)

	20 Apr	15 Jun	21 Sep	18 Dec
ADB's developing members[a]	1,841,936	2,958,468	3,577,102	3,627,976
Central and West Asia	31,547	34,995	45,341	47,659
East Asia	1,456,564	2,234,199	2,730,910	2,738,440
Pacific	2,213	2,465	2,579	2,602
South Asia	72,798	360,000	391,050	428,505
Southeast Asia	278,813	326,810	407,222	410,770
Other ADB members[b]	9,411,332	14,052,615	16,092,795	17,513,283
ECB and EU	4,358,804	5,249,730	5,694,129	6,268,613
Total	15,612,073	22,260,813	25,364,026	27,409,871

ADB = Asian Development Bank, COVID-19 = coronavirus disease, ECB = European Central Bank, EU = European Union.

Notes:

[a] Central and West Asia: Afghanistan, Armenia, Azerbaijan, Georgia, Kazakhstan, the Kyrgyz Republic, Pakistan, Uzbekistan. East Asia: Hong Kong, China; Mongolia; the People's Republic of China; the Republic of Korea; Taipei,China. South Asia: Bangladesh, Bhutan, India, Maldives, Sri Lanka. Southeast Asia: Brunei Darussalam, Cambodia, Indonesia, the Lao People's Democratic Republic, Malaysia, Myanmar, the Philippines, Singapore, Thailand, Timor-Leste, Viet Nam. Pacific: the Cook Islands, the Federated States of Micronesia, Fiji, the Marshall Islands, Nauru, Palau, Papua New Guinea, Samoa, Solomon Islands, Tonga, Tuvalu, Vanuatu. Only one country in the Pacific, Niue, has not publicly announced any specific amount to combat COVID-19 and is thus excluded from this table.

[b] Other ADB members: Australia, Austria, Belgium, Canada, Denmark, Finland, France, Germany, Ireland, Italy, Japan, Luxembourg, the Netherlands, New Zealand, Norway, Portugal, Spain, Sweden, Switzerland, Turkey, the United Kingdom, and the United States.

Source: Authors' calculations based on data from the ADB COVID-19 Policy Database at https://covid19policy.adb.org.

Table 9 shows the countries with the largest packages in absolute value across the four selected dates. The top 10 countries are the same across the observed dates, with the exception of India as of 20 April 2020, when it was ranked 20th. The total packages have stabilized as of 21 September 2020, except for Canada, whose package still increased by 39.3% between 21 September and 18 December 2020. As of 18 December 2020, four countries accounted for over half of the global package. These are the US ($8.1 trillion), Japan ($3.4 trillion), the PRC ($2.3 trillion), and Germany ($2.1 trillion). Of the top 10 countries, only two—the PRC and India—are developing countries. The largest increases between 20 April and 18 December 2020 belong to India (544.6%), Japan (195.2%), and Canada (188.1%).

Table 9. Top 10 Economies with the Largest Packages, as of 20 April, 15 June, 21 September, and 18 December 2020
($ million)

Rank	Economies	20 Apr	15 Jun	21 Sep	18 Dec
1	United States	4,446,634	6,038,993	7,084,712	8,061,391
2	Japan	1,163,476	3,091,993	3,431,272	3,434,282
3	People's Republic of China	1,148,817	2,020,020	2,260,396	2,317,391
4	Germany	1,837,389	2,008,827	2,053,796	2,130,190
5	Canada	296,130	609,148	612,453	853,245
6	United Kingdom	719,440	837,129	834,838	840,651
7	France	509,469	547,511	760,355	783,119
8	Italy	504,408	568,302	709,663	711,018
9	India	63,933	350,982	376,389	412,092
10	Australia	199,632	260,511	357,200	383,340

Note: Ranking is based on 18 December 2020 packages.

Source: Authors' calculations based on data from the ADB COVID-19 Policy Database at https://covid19policy.adb.org.

Table 10 shows the top five packages per capita and as a percentage of GDP as of 20 April and 18 December 2020, for both ADB's developing members and other ADB members, ranked according to the 18 December 2020 package. The packages of Hong Kong, China and Singapore led ADB's developing members at 52.1% and 24.6% of GDP, respectively, as of 18 December 2020. Meanwhile, Japan and Germany led the other ADB members at 66.6% and 55.1%, respectively. In terms of package per capita, Hong Kong, China provided the highest amount at $25,898, followed by Singapore at $15,629. Among the other ADB members, Luxembourg and Japan provided the largest packages at $29,046 and $27,199, respectively.

Table 10. Top Five Economies with the Largest Packages as a Percentage of Gross Domestic Product and per Capita, as of 20 April and 18 December 2020

ADB's Developing Members		20 Apr	18 Dec	Other ADB Members		20 Apr	18 Dec
% of GDP							
1	Hong Kong, China	47.4	52.1	1	Japan	22.6	66.6
2	Singapore	19.0	24.6	2	Germany	47.6	55.1
3	Malaysia	16.6	22.1	3	Finland	48.1	53.7
4	Marshall Islands	3.2	19.1	4	Canada	17.1	49.3
5	Mongolia	14.5	18.2	5	United States	20.7	37.6
Per capita ($)							
1	Hong Kong, China	23,567	25,898	1	Luxembourg	17,131	29,046
2	Singapore	12,061	15,629	2	Japan	9,215	27,199
3	Republic of Korea	2,445	4,799	3	Finland	23,496	26,236
4	Malaysia	1,894	2,528	4	Germany	22,102	25,624
5	Taipei,China	422	2,053	5	Switzerland	16,254	25,213

ADB = Asian Development Bank, GDP = gross domestic product.

Note: Ranking is based on 18 December 2020 packages.

Source: Authors' calculations based on data from the ADB COVID-19 Policy Database at https://covid19policy.adb.org and ADB *Asian Development Outlook 2020* database for Cook Islands' GDP and population.

B.   What Measures Did ADB Members Implement?

This section provides details on the composition of the packages by type of measure. Figure 2 (ADB developing members) and Figure 3 (other ADB members) show a breakdown of the packages into the sum of Measures 01–04, Measure 05, and Measure 10, with Measure 02C specifically segregated. The overall composition of the packages has remained fairly constant over time for both ADB's developing members and the other ADB members. As of 18 December 2020, ADB's developing members devoted more to Measure 05 (50.8% of the total) than to the sum of Measures 01–04 (46.7% of the total including Measure 02C); while the reverse is true for the other ADB members, with Measures 01–04 consistently accounting for the majority of the total package, averaging 60% of the total across the four dates. Comparing amounts in Measure 02C between ADB developing members and other ADB members, the latter dedicated substantially more to loan guarantees, both as a percentage of the total and in absolute amounts.

As of 18 December 2020, Measures 01–04 added up to $1.7 trillion for ADB's developing members and $10.2 trillion for the other ADB members (a total of $16.1 trillion including the ECB and the EU), representing 7.1% and 21.3% of their combined GDPs, respectively. On the other hand,

Figure 2. ADB Developing Members' Packages, as of 20 April, 15 June, 21 September, and 18 December 2020
(Package amounts and % of total)

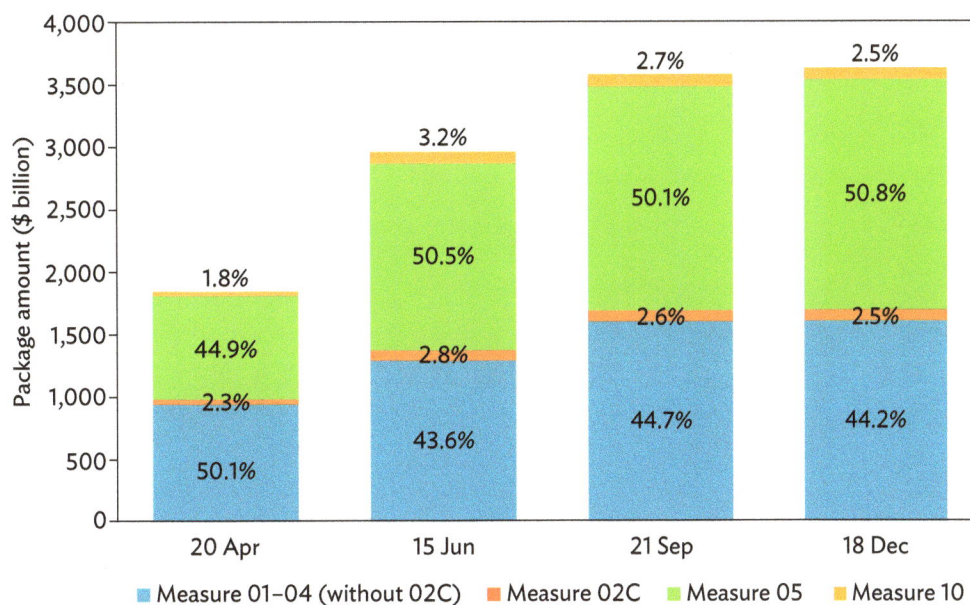

ADB = Asian Development Bank.

Notes: The measures are grouped together to capture the financial positions that central banks and governments have taken relative to the private sector and state or local governments. Measures 01–04 except 02C consist of liquidity support, credit creation, direct long-term lending, and equity support, while Measure 02C consists of loan guarantees. Measure 05 and Measure 10 consist of health and income support and no breakdown, respectively.

Source: Authors' calculations based on data from the ADB COVID-19 Policy Database at https://covid19policy.adb.org.

Measure 05 was at $1.8 trillion for ADB's developing members and $7.2 trillion for other ADB members, equivalent to 7.7% and 14.9% of their combined GDPs, respectively.[17]

Table 11 provides further details by type of measure (columns) for each region or economy (rows). Credit creation and health and income support make up most of the total package of all 68 ADB members (including the ECB and the EU). These two measures account for 46.9% and 32.9% of the total, respectively. These shares vary between ADB's developing members and other ADB members: in the former, the share of credit creation is 16% and that of health and income support is 50.8%; in the latter, the share of credit creation is 51.6% and that of health and income support is 30.1%.

---

[17]   As of 20 May 2020, the International Monetary Fund's estimate of the global fiscal support amounted to $9 trillion (Battersby, Lam, and Ture 2020). While this includes direct budget support (corresponding to Measure 05), it also includes public sector loans and equity injections, guarantees, and other actions (such as noncommercial activity of public corporations) that have different impacts on the financial positions of the government and nongovernment sectors compared to health and income support. Interestingly, as of 29 June 2020, the Center for Strategic and International Studies estimated the total fiscal package of the G20 countries at $7.6 trillion, representing 11.2% of their aggregated GDP (Segal and Dylan 2020).

Figure 3. Other ADB Members' Packages, as of 20 April, 15 June, 21 September, and 18 December 2020
(Package amounts and % of total)

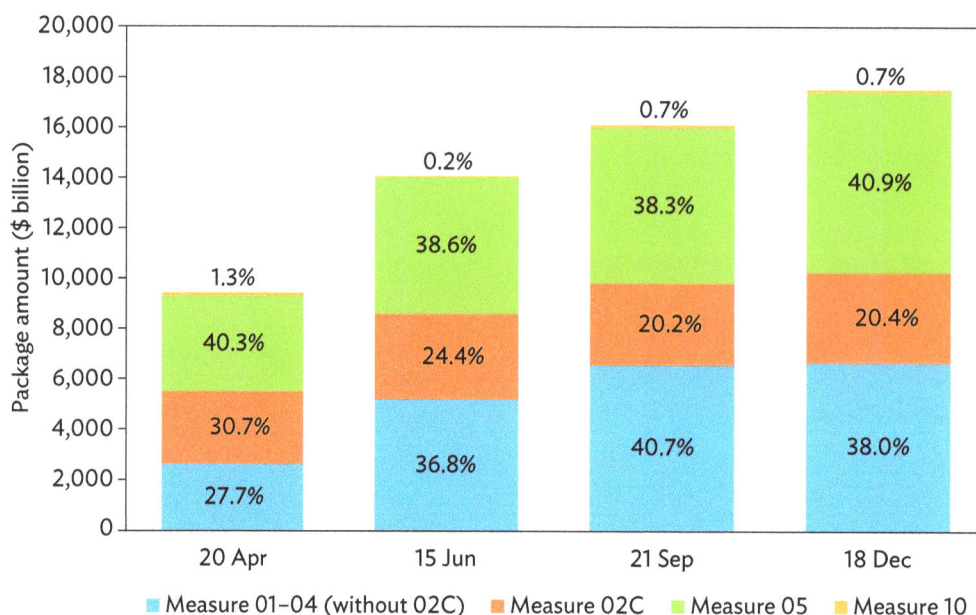

ADB = Asian Development Bank.

Notes: The measures are grouped together to capture the financial positions that central banks and governments have taken relative to the private sector and state or local governments. Measures 01–04 except 02C consist of liquidity support, credit creation, direct long-term lending, and equity support, while Measure 02C consists of loan guarantees. Measure 05 and Measure 10 consist of health and income support and no breakdown, respectively.

Source: Authors' calculations based on data from the ADB COVID-19 Policy Database at https://covid19policy.adb.org.

ADB's developing members allocated the largest share of their packages to health and income support. In Central and West Asia, this share was 62.2% as of 18 December 2020. The second-largest measure varies across the regions. In East Asia and South Asia, liquidity support is the next largest measure, while direct long-term lending is the next largest measure in Central and West Asia, Southeast Asia, and the Pacific.

As a group, the smallest shares in both ADB developing members and other ADB members are direct long-term lending and equity support to the private sector: combined, they make up only 9.1% of ADB developing members' total package, and 6.6% of the other ADB members' total package. Southeast Asia is the only region that allocated a noticeably larger share to direct long-term lending—29.7% of the total package. The share of equity support to the private sector is very small in both ADB developing members and other ADB members.

Table 11. Share of Each Measure in Total Packages, as of 18 December 2020
(%)

	Liquidity Support (01)	Credit Creation (02)	Direct Long-Term Lending (03)	Equity Support (04)	Health and Income Support (05)	No Breakdown (10)
All ADB members	11.1	46.9	5.5	1.4	32.9	2.2
ADB's developing members	21.6	16.0	7.9	1.2	50.8	2.5
Central and West Asia	12.8	9.4	13.0	–	62.2	2.6
East Asia	21.2	16.6	5.7	1.5	52.2	2.8
South Asia	38.2	15.0	0.1	–	46.6	0.1
Southeast Asia	8.0	13.9	29.7	1.2	44.6	2.7
Pacific	–	1.0	9.0	–	39.3	50.6
Other ADB members	9.5	51.6	5.2	1.4	30.1	2.2
United States	6.2	50.4	10.6	–	32.8	–
Japan	27.2	2.9	–	3.3	66.6	–

– = not available, ADB = Asian Development Bank.

Notes: The percentages shown for each group (i.e., rows for all members, developing members and regions, and other members) are computed by summing the measures (numerator) and total packages (denominator) of all economies belonging in the aggregation. For the United States and Japan, Measure 09 is excluded in their total packages.

Source: Authors' calculations based on data from the ADB COVID-19 Policy Database at https://covid19policy.adb.org.

The following are some remarks on each measure:

01. Liquidity support. This measure aims to provide short-term liquidity to ensure the normal functioning of money markets. Actions include short-term lending to the private sector, regulatory adjustments to liquidity requirements, and foreign exchange operations.

Among ADB's developing members, India and Hong Kong, China have allocated significant shares of their total packages to this measure at 38.6% and 66.8%, respectively. India's actions included increased short-term repurchase agreements (0.1% of GDP); variable-term repurchase agreements (0.5% of GDP); and special refinance facilities for rural banks, housing finance companies, and small enterprises (0.2% of GDP). On the other hand, Hong Kong, China's actions relied more heavily on relaxing liquidity requirements with an estimated $129.8 billion in lending capacity released through the reduction in regulatory reserves.[18] These two members, plus the PRC, account for over 91% of

---

[18] This is an example of how some economies have reported monetary values on regulatory items in Measures 01B and 02B. For Measure 01B, the estimation appears to be similar to a money multiplier view of how much relaxed reserve requirements might increase excess reserves available for credit creation. For Measure 02B, the calculations are linked to how much additional balance sheet space becomes available when capital requirements are relaxed. The vast majority of economies relaxed regulatory measures related to both Measures 01B and 02B, but only a small minority reported estimates for potential credit creation that might result.

the total amount allocated to Measure 01 by ADB's developing members. In terms of growth over time, the largest percentage increases from 20 April to 18 December 2020 for ADB's developing members were registered by Georgia (766%), India (712.2%), and Bangladesh (660%). For Georgia, the majority of this increase occurred between 21 September and 18 December 2020, while India and Bangladesh allocated most of their packages between 20 April and 15 June 2020. The largest absolute increases across all four dates in 2020 were registered by the PRC, India, and Hong Kong, China. As of 18 December 2020, the measure accounted for 18.5%, 38.6%, and 66.8% of their respective total packages.

Among the other ADB members, Switzerland consistently maintains the highest allocation to this measure as a percentage of its total package across all four dates, reaching 48.3% as of 18 December 2020. Japan is a far second at 27%, followed by Germany (23.7%) and Canada (21.9%). The vast majority of Switzerland's actions under Measure 01 were in foreign exchange operations totaling more than $100 billion in order to keep the Swiss franc from appreciating. In contrast, Canada's actions in Measure 01, which was $187 billion (21.9% of the total package) as of 18 December 2020, include no foreign exchange operations due to Canada's freely floating exchange rate. Instead, it includes Bank of Canada purchases of banker's acceptances, short-term debt of the provinces, and commercial paper; multiple repurchase agreement facilities at the Bank of Canada; and short-term loans from government agencies to small businesses, nonprofit organizations, and farms. Finally, the UK and Switzerland registered the largest percentage increases in this measure among the other ADB members, with most of the increases occurring between 20 April and 15 June 2020.

02. Credit creation. This measure aims to encourage the financial sector to increase provision of credit to the nonfinancial private sector and to subnational governments. Actions under this measure include loans to the financial sector, secondary market purchases, provision of loan guarantees, interest rate reductions, and other regulatory adjustments. From 20 April to 18 December 2020, Pakistan registered the highest growth in the amount allocated to this measure among the developing members at 432.6%, followed by the PRC (337.9%) and India (307.2%). Bangladesh and Thailand allocated significant shares of their total packages to this measure across the four dates in 2020. As of 18 December 2020, this measure accounted for 31.6% and 31.5% of their respective total packages. The Bank of Thailand offered $15.6 billion in loans to financial institutions to finance lending to small and medium-sized enterprises (SMEs). Bangladesh subsidized interest payments of up to $5.9 billion in working capital loans by scheduled banks to businesses.

Among the other ADB members, the ECB, Italy, and Belgium had the highest allocations to this measure across the four dates in 2020. Both Italy and Belgium implemented state guarantee programs for bank loans, as well as reinsurance schemes, accounting for nearly 67.1% and 82.4% of their respective total packages. Practically the entire package of the ECB is in Measure 02. As of 18 December 2020, it has been offering "Targeted Longer-Term Refinancing Operations" to financial institutions at negative interest rates, estimating that this could enable the equivalent of 3 trillion euros (€) in private credit creation. Another program, the ECB's Pandemic Emergency Purchase Programme, was authorized for another €1.35 trillion in security purchases. Aside from the ECB, the US allocated $3.6 trillion (as of 18 December 2020) to this measure. It includes several of the new standing facilities of the Federal Reserve, such as the Paycheck Protection Program Lending Facility, the Secondary Market Credit Facility, the Main Street New Loan Facility, and the reestablished Term Asset-Backed Securities Loan Facility, as well as increased purchases of mortgage-backed securities.[19] It also includes nearly $1.1 trillion in guarantees provided by the government to banks and to the Federal Reserve. Since the first reporting date on 20 April 2020, the largest growth in credit creation for other ADB members was registered by Japan (425%), followed by Canada (273.1%) and the US (237.3%). In these three cases, most of the increase occurred between 20 April and 15 June 2020, with minimal increments between 15 June and 18 December 2020.

03. Direct long-term lending. This measure consists of long-term loans to the nonfinancial private sector as well as forbearances. The Republic of Korea (ROK) consistently leads ADB's developing members in absolute amounts allocated to this measure, which reached $106.2 billion as of 18 December 2020, comprising 42.8% of its total package. Some of the specific measures it has implemented include expanded lending and new bond purchasing facilities. Among the other ADB members, the US and the EU allocated the largest absolute amounts, accounting for 9.9% and 29.1% of their total packages, respectively. In the US, the Federal Reserve established the Municipal Liquidity Facility, which will offer up to $500 billion in lending to states and municipalities to manage cash flow stresses caused by the COVID-19 pandemic, while the US government offered loans to businesses critical to national security and also for emergency disaster relief. The EU established the Pandemic Crisis Support credit lines, with access granted for up to 2% of an EU country's GDP as of end of 2019.

04. Equity support. At just over 1% of all ADB members' total package, this measure is the smallest of the first five measures. Among ADB's developing members, Singapore and the ROK allocated the highest amounts to this measure as a percentage of the total package, reaching 4.2% and 3.8% of their respective total packages. Notably, both countries infused equity funds into their flag carriers, Singapore Airlines and Korean Air. Among other ADB members, Germany allocated the highest absolute amount, spending $133.3 billion to directly acquire equity of affected companies (e.g., Lufthansa). Japan, on the other hand, increased purchases of exchange-traded funds and Japan Real Estate Investment Trusts by $111.8 billion (2.2% of GDP) and $1.7 billion (0.03% of GDP), respectively. Interestingly, the US has not yet allocated anything to this measure, in contrast with its Troubled Asset Relief Program that purchased private equity positions in large financial institutions during the 2008 GFC.

05. Health and income support. This measure reflects both health and nonhealth government expenditure designed to increase income and improve the financial positions (net worth) of the private sector. Nonhealth expenditure is further subdivided into tax policy changes, wage support to individuals, business subsidies, and indirect income support (e.g., funding for culture, infrastructure, environment, and other expenditures with multiplier effects).

Among ADB developing members, the PRC and India allocated the largest amounts to this measure, $1.3 trillion (56.4% of total package) and $194.4 billion (47.2% of total package), respectively.

---

[19] The $3.6 trillion figure uses the authorized amounts for the Secondary Market Credit Facility (included with the Primary Market Credit Facility, since the Federal Reserve uses the same Special Purpose Vehicle [SPV] to lend to both facilities and then reports at the level of this vehicle rather than the individual facilities), the Main Street New Loan Facility, and the Term Asset-Backed Securities Lending Facility, all of which total $1.45 trillion.

Major nonhealth spending for the PRC includes local government infrastructure projects, tax relief and waived social security contributions, interest concessions, and price reductions, with notably little in the way of direct income support to households and individuals (less than 1% of the total package). This is in contrast to India, where direct income support makes up 10.9% of the total package and is the largest absolute amount within this category. Other actions implemented by India include subsidies for businesses, investments in health institutions, and programs for the agriculture sector. For the rest of ADB developing members, each economy prioritized a different expenditure category, usually having little to no allocation for the other categories. For instance, Viet Nam allocated 30.2% of its total package to tax and contribution deferrals, and Georgia allocated 19.4% of its total package to tax and contribution rate reductions. Afghanistan and Tajikistan prioritized income support to individuals (79.1% and 57.4% of their total packages, respectively), while Mongolia and Nauru mainly used business subsidies. On the other hand, Uzbekistan and Tuvalu allocated the largest percentage of their total package to health expenditures at 96.8% and 89%, respectively. From 20 April to 18 December 2020, ADB developing members registered large increases in health and income support. In terms of absolute amounts, the PRC and India grew the most, with increases totaling $737.5 billion and $164.3 billion, respectively, during this period.

Japan and the US allocated the largest amounts to this measure at $2.3 trillion each (66.1% and 28.8% of their respective total packages). Japan launched the Emergency Economic Package Against COVID-19, which represents 43.4% of its GDP (as of 18 December 2020). Some of the measures it has implemented include health-related initiatives, support to businesses and households, and transfers to the local governments. Meanwhile, the US has enacted five major laws to implement its fiscal packages: Coronavirus Preparedness and Response Supplemental Appropriations Act; Families First Coronavirus Response Act; Coronavirus Aid, Relief, and Economic Security (CARES) Act; Paycheck Protection Program and Healthcare Enhancement Act (PPPHCEA); and a $900 billion relief bill signed into law on 27 December 2020. As of 18 December 2020, nonhealth expenditures for the other ADB members were distributed across multiple nonhealth expenditures, in contrast with ADB developing members who allocated much of their expenditures under this measure to a single category. For example, Austria allocated 41.9% of its total package to business subsidies and also allocated substantial amounts to wage support to individuals and tax and contribution deferrals. Australia and the US allocated the most to health expenditures at 22.9% and 7.6% of their total packages, respectively. In absolute amounts, Japan leads the other ADB members with an increase of $1.3 trillion from 20 April to 18 December 2020, followed by the US at $1 trillion. Much of this $1 trillion increase in the US package came from the latest stimulus package. Table 12 shows a partial breakdown.

Table 12. Partial Breakdown of the United States' December 2020 Stimulus Package

Measure	Amount	Details
Loan guarantees	$284 billion	Additional $284 billion for forgivable Paycheck Protection Program loan
Health	$54 billion	(a) $20 billion for the purchase of vaccines, (b) $9 billion for vaccine distribution, (c) $22 billion to assist states with testing, and (d) $3 billion for the National Strategic Stockpile of vaccines
Support to individuals and households	$337.9 billion	(a) $25 billion in rental assistance for individuals that have lost their source of income during the pandemic; (b) $400 million to food banks and food pantries through the Emergency Food Assistance Program; (c) $175 million for nutrition services for seniors and $13 million for the Commodity Supplemental Food Program, which services more than 700,000 older Americans monthly; (d) $13 billion to raise Supplemental Nutritional Assistance Program (SNAP) benefits by 15% for 6 months while not expanding eligibility; (e) $168 billion in direct payment checks of up to $600 per adult and child; (f) $128 billion in additional unemployment insurance benefits of $300 per week; (g) $2 billion for states to help families with coronavirus-related funeral expenses; and (h) $1.3 billion to forgive federal loans to historically Black colleges and universities and deliver grants to incarcerated students (ending a 26-year ban)
Support to businesses	$73 billion	(a) $10 billion to support childcare providers; (b) $15 billion to airlines to help maintain their payrolls; (c) $13 billion for farmers and ranchers to help cover pandemic-induced losses; (d) $20 billion for businesses in low-income communities; and (e) $15 billion for struggling live venues, movie theaters, and museums
Indirect income support	$116.3 billion	(a) $82 billion to schools and colleges, (b) $7 billion to bolster broadband access to help Americans connect remotely during the pandemic, (c) $10 billion for state highways, (d) $1 billion for Amtrak, (e) $14 billion for mass transit, and (f) $2.3 billion to the military for a second Virginia-class attack submarine

Source: Raju, Manu, and Clare Foran. 2020. "Hill Leaders Reach $900 Billion Covid Relief Deal in Breakthrough following Partisan Disputes." *CNN*. 20 December. https://edition.cnn.com/2020/12/20/politics/stimulus-latest-shutdown-deadline.

The multiple COVID-19 relief acts in the US are a good example of how actual allocations to Measure 05 can differ from the headline monetary values of government legislation. The CARES Act has a total value of $2.2 trillion, but includes nearly $775 billion in guarantees (Measure 02C) to banks (in the PPPHCEA) and to the Federal Reserve, as well as smaller allocations for loans to private businesses (Measures 01A and 03A). Similarly, the PPPHCEA is nearly $500 billion, but includes $321 billion for loan guarantees and another $50 billion in emergency disaster relief loans to small businesses. The four legislative acts combine for $2.9 trillion, but the portion of this that applies to Measure 05 is $1.7 trillion.

09. International assistance. This measure includes the provision of currency swaps and loans among central banks, as well as donations and grants. The Federal Reserve is by far the largest provider of central bank currency swaps given its contractual agreements with 14 other central banks. Central bank currency swap lines were also provided by the central banks of the EU, India, Japan, the PRC, the ROK, and Singapore. In some instances, the Federal Reserve and the ECB also provided lines of credit secured by government securities in their respective currencies, in lieu of loans secured by the borrowing nations' currencies. Meanwhile, other ADB members, along with the PRC and the ROK, also engaged in direct international assistance, either through direct transfers to intended beneficiaries or increased contributions to multilateral organizations.

C.   How Were the Measures Funded?

Economies can fund the implementation of their packages through (i) central bank financing, (ii) international assistance as a borrower or recipient, and (iii) reallocating previously budgeted government spending.

First, any lending or purchasing actions of the central banks in Measures 01–04 in domestic currency are inherently self-funded, since these actions simply involve a central bank crediting the account of the bank if the bank is the counterparty, or if the counterparty is not a bank, then the central bank can credit the account of the counterparty's bank, who then credits the counterparty's account.

For government deficit positions, central banks are the major funding sources in the UK, Canada, and the US, where this source is equivalent to about 20.5%, 13.5%, and 10.7% of their respective GDPs. Most of this comes from secondary market purchases of government bonds. Direct lending to governments is much more uncommon, which is only used by Canada, Indonesia, the Philippines, Singapore, and the US.[20] In the case of the Philippines, this was accomplished through a $5.9 billion repurchase agreement from the central bank to the government, while the Indonesian central bank opted to purchase sharia sovereign bonds through a government auction in the primary market.

A second source of funding, international assistance (Measure 08), comes mostly from the network of central bank bilateral swap agreements and via temporary repo facilities (the latter provided independently by the Federal Reserve and the ECB to central banks in emerging market economies against the risk-free collateral in the lender's currency). Among ADB's developing members, those securing swap lines and/or liquidity facilities from multiple central banks include Indonesia, the ROK, Singapore, and Hong Kong, China.

---

[20] The US case here is unique, involving the government's backstop of Federal Reserve lending programs, as authorized in the CARES Act. As of 27 July 2020, $114 billion has been moved from the Treasury's account on the Federal Reserve's balance sheet into "special" accounts that are effectively equity investments in the Federal Reserve's SPVs. Of this amount, $96 billion is invested directly in nonmarketable domestic series US government debt. In other words, $96 billion of the government's current $114 billion equity position in the Federal Reserve's SPVs is invested directly in newly issued, nonmarketable US government securities. To be more precise, $1.5 billion of the $114 billion is allocated to the Federal Reserve Money Market Liquidity Facility, which is not among the Federal Reserve's SPVs.

Other forms of international assistance come from ADB and other multilateral organizations such as the World Bank, the International Monetary Fund, and the Asian Infrastructure Investment Bank, but these make up a small share overall. Nevertheless, international assistance remains an important source of funds for small economies such as those in the Pacific, where it amounts to about 3.8% of the region's total GDP, compared to 0.2% for the rest of ADB's developing members. Meanwhile, in absolute amounts, India received the most assistance at $5.9 billion, followed by Indonesia at $5.1 billion.

Lastly, reallocating previously budgeted government spending has been the least used financing measure. Among all ADB members, only Indonesia and the EU have used this measure.

D.   Conclusions

As we look back on how economies responded to the COVID-19 pandemic during the past year, one thing has become clear: extraordinary crises require equally extraordinary measures. As early as April 2020, ADB members, led by economies such as Japan, the PRC, and the US, as well as the ECB and the EU, had already announced packages totaling $15.6 trillion. By the end of the year, this increased by 76% to $27.4 trillion. This amount consisted of a wide variety of measures, with economies showing both similarities and differences in their approaches to curbing the effects of the crisis. Analyzing the amount and composition of the packages reveals that ADB developing members allocated the largest share of their packages to health and income support (Measure 05) at 50.8%, while the other ADB members allocated more to credit creation (Measure 02) at 51.6%.

Chapter IV

Quantitative and Qualitative Comparison of Packages for Selected Asian Countries

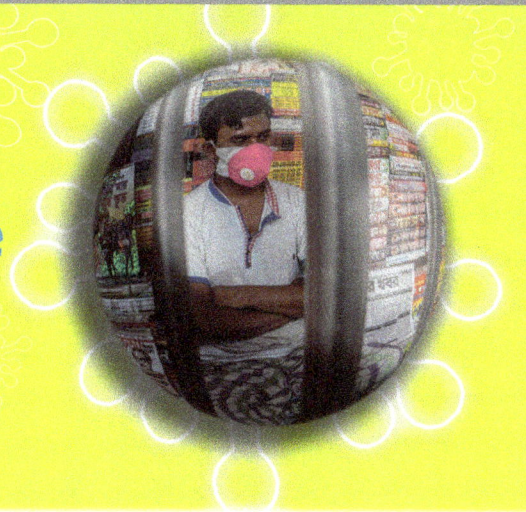

This chapter provides an analysis of qualitative and quantitative differences in the COVID-19 response packages of the Philippines, Indonesia, Thailand, Malaysia, the ROK, and Singapore. The objective is to go into some more detail in order to compare and contrast policy responses across these countries. Section IV.A discusses the monetary values of the countries' respective packages for each measure. Section IV.B looks qualitatively at the various ways they responded through Measures 01, 02, and 03. Section IV.C discusses how the countries' respective central banks acted to support government financing of deficits related to the COVID-19 policy responses.

A. The Monetary Values of the Countries' COVID-19 Relief Packages

Table 13 shows the estimated or authorized monetary values of the packages as a percentage of GDP reported by each of the six countries for Measures 01–05 and 10. Cells in Measures 01–03 highlight in parentheses some of the similarities or differences of the measures across countries. Positive values in Measure 10 for Malaysia and the ROK imply that some announced policies in these countries were not clear enough to determine which combination of measures within Measures 01–05 they belonged to. For Malaysia, there appear to be some actions that could fit into all five measures; whereas for the ROK, the actions appear to fit Measures 02, 03, and 04 but with no clear delineation of how much for each. The final two rows list the countries' packages as a percentage of GDP and in US dollars per capita.

Table 13. Monetary Values of Policy Measures as a Percentage of Gross Domestic Product for the Philippines, Indonesia, Thailand, Malaysia, the Republic of Korea, and Singapore, as of 18 December 2020

Measure	Philippines	Indonesia	Thailand	Malaysia	Republic of Korea	Singapore
01 Liquidity support	1.4 (entirely for lower reserve and liquidity requirements)	1.4 (0.7 for lower reserve and liquidity requirements)	– (actions, but no amounts)	2.9 (1.0 for lower reserve requirements)	1.1	0.8
02 Credit creation	0.6 (entirely for loan guarantees)	1.6 (entirely for loan guarantees)	5.0 (2.1 for loan guarantees)	3.3 (entirely for loan guarantees)	– (guarantees, but no amounts)	–
03 Direct lending	0.2	4.3	2.7	7.2 (6.6 for forbearances)	6.8	6.0
04 Equity support	–	–	–	0.1	0.6	1.1
05 Health and income support	3.7	3.6	8.3	6.8	4.3	14.7
10 No breakdown	–	–	–	2.5	2.1	–
Total as a percentage of GDP	5.9	10.9	16.0	22.7	15.0	22.5
Total in US dollars ($) per capita	200	426	1,208	2,528	4,539	13,872

– = not available, GDP = gross domestic product, US = United States.

Source: Asian Development Bank. ADB COVID-19 Policy Database. https://covid19policy.adb.org.

In all six countries, Measures 01, 02, and 03 have some versions of the following: (i) relaxed certain liquidity (01B) and capital requirements (02B2); (ii) relaxed regulatory oversight to enable banks to restructure or defer customers' loans (02B2, 03B); and (iii) reduced central bank interest rate targets (02B1). These are important actions that unfortunately do not translate easily into monetary amounts for reporting (this is the topic of a more qualitative analysis in section IV.B). Nevertheless, a relatively small minority of countries did report monetary amounts for one or more of these, including, coincidentally, half of this sample (Indonesia, Malaysia, and the Philippines), all for relaxed liquidity requirements (01B). On the other hand, the ROK, Singapore, and Thailand reported actions but no accompanying monetary amounts for Measures 01B and 02C (loan guarantees).

The packages for the Philippines and Indonesia are substantially smaller as a percentage of GDP and in per capita terms than the other four countries, with the Philippines' package roughly half of that of Indonesia's. Both have comparatively smaller amounts for Measures 02 and 03 combined (except for Singapore, whose Measures 02 and 03 are about the same size as Indonesia's), and relatively smaller values for Measure 05. Half of the amount reported by Indonesia under Measure 01, as noted in Table 13, is for reduced liquidity requirements that provide additional liquidity (about 22 trillion rupiah [Rp]) and fewer "demand deposit obligations" (about Rp96 trillion). The former refers to traditional bank reserve requirements, while the latter refers to more recent macroprudential liquidity regulations. Further, Bank Indonesia (BI) also raised a separate liquidity requirement for banks—the "liquidity buffer ratio"—that could only be fulfilled via government bond purchases in the primary market, for which no monetary amounts were reported. The Philippines' Bangko Sentral ng Pilipinas (BSP) reported the entire amount under Measure 01 as an increase in liquidity available due to reduced requirements in Measure 01B. However, the BSP also carried out increased open market operations in March 2020 (the most severe period of liquidity difficulties) that were later reversed by a nearly equal amount to that reported in Measure 01B. This suggests that instead of Measure 01 being larger for the Philippines and Indonesia than for the other countries in Table 13, it is more likely smaller or at least not larger than the others, consistent with their comparatively smaller packages overall.

At first sight, the packages for Thailand and Malaysia seem quite different, with Malaysia's larger than Thailand's by more than $1,320 per capita. But a deeper look suggests their sizes are probably more similar. Recall that Thailand reported actions but not monetary amounts for Measure 01. If we assume these actions amounted to about 1% of GDP—about the average of the next two smallest entries for Measure 01 in the table (1.1% of GDP for the ROK and 0.8% of GDP for Singapore)—this would add about $75 per capita to Thailand's package. Malaysia's Bank Negara Malaysia (BNM), like the BSP and BI, incorporated monetary amounts for Measure 01B that equal about $117 per capita. Further, Malaysia's entry for Measure 03 (7.2% of GDP) is mostly due to its inclusion of a monetary estimate of 6.6% of GDP for Measure 03B (forbearances), which is the impact of a 6-month moratorium and restructuring for small and medium-sized enterprises (SMEs). Thailand likewise reports a "loan payment holiday of 6 months for SMEs and suspension of principal" for Measure 03, but like most countries, it does not report a monetary value. The forbearance entry for Malaysia is worth about $735 per capita. Taken together, these would decrease the $1,320 per capita difference between the two countries' packages to $393 per capita.[21]

The ROK's package is the second largest in the table in per capita terms. Two things stand out—the smaller percentage than those of Malaysia, Singapore, and Thailand for Measure 05 and the lack of a monetary amount for Measure 02. On Measure 02, the ADB database notes that there are loan guarantees under this measure, but their value is a portion of the entry in Measure 05. The database

---

[21] If Malaysia's package is closer to Thailand's in terms of size per capita, then this would be consistent with the results in Table 20 that suggest that Malaysia's reported package is significantly larger than the models predict. The same does not hold for Thailand, for which the regressions also predict much lower values. As a potential explanation for this, the notes for Measure 05 for Thailand in the ADB COVID-19 Policy Database report a deliberate attempt by Thailand's government to pass a fiscal package of 10% of GDP, which is a clear anomaly in the database, especially for ADB member economies. (The database reports a value less than 10% of GDP for Thailand's Measure 05 because some parts do not fit the database's definition of "income support" and instead appear in Measures 02 and 03.)

also reports loan guarantees within the collection of actions in the entry for Measure 10. Of course, this does not increase the size of the ROK's total package (the combined sum of Measures 01 through 05 and 10—excluding Measure 09 for this section's discussion), and the loan guarantees that are part of Measure 05 mean that the ROK is devoting even less to health and income support than the already relatively small amount shown in the cell (4.3% of GDP). Overall, and given that the ROK's entry for Measure 10 most likely cannot be added to Measure 05, the ROK's response to COVID-19 puts the most emphasis of the five countries on loan guarantees, lending to or refinancing the private sector, corporate bond purchases, and (to a lesser extent) increasing equity claims of the government or central bank on the private sector, while it puts the least emphasis on health and income support to the private sector.

Singapore's package is more than triple the size of the ROK's in per capita terms. Interestingly, as a percentage of GDP, it is nearly the same size as Malaysia's package, both of which are about 50% larger than the ROK's package (Malaysia's reporting of monetary values for Measures 01B and 03B notwithstanding). While Singapore's package has significant values for Measures 03 and 04 relative to the other countries, what sets Singapore apart is Measure 05's contribution at 14.7% of GDP, which is roughly two-thirds of the country's total package.

Finally, even as the discussion in this section suggested that monetary values for certain measures, such as Measures 01B, 02B, and 03B, might be inflating the estimated packages of the Philippines, Indonesia, and particularly Malaysia, it is important to note that this is only because the majority of countries did not report monetary estimates for these measures. In other words, there is not an objectively "correct" standard—it could very well be that reporting such estimates is more appropriate and that other countries' packages are instead underestimated. The ADB database therefore makes no judgment on this and simply accounts for what is reported by the respective countries.

B.   Qualitative Comparison of Measures 01, 02, and 03

To assist in understanding and comparing the first three measures, the qualitative complements to Table 13's presentation of Measures 01, 02, and 03 are presented in Tables 14, 15, and 16, respectively, which include the various actions taken for each of the measure's submeasures.

Measure 01—provision of liquidity and short-term refinance—is separated into actual lending or asset purchase actions (01A), reserve and liquidity-related requirements (01B), and foreign currency operations or requirements (01C). As Table 14 shows, five of the six countries increased the volume of normal open market operations, while Thailand did not report a change. The Philippines' BSP temporarily cancelled its term auction facility operations and its overnight reverse repurchase operations, both of which drain reserve balances. All six provided liquidity facilities to their respective banking sectors. Malaysia, the ROK, and Singapore offered such facilities to other financial institutions and businesses. Malaysia and the ROK offered loans to certain SMEs. Malaysia's BNM provided additional special relief facilities to fund working capital needs to agrofood and automation or digitalization of SMEs. The ROK purchased commercial paper and also offered short-term loans to the automobile industry

Table 14. Comparison of Measure 01 for the Philippines, Indonesia, Thailand, Malaysia, the Republic of Korea, and Singapore, as of 18 December 2020

	Measure	Philippines	Indonesia	Thailand	Malaysia	Republic of Korea	Singapore
01A	Increased volume of normal open market operations	Yes	Yes		Yes	Yes	Yes
	Reduced normal operations that drain central bank reserve balances	Yes					
	Liquidity facilities—bank sector	Yes	Yes	Yes	Yes	Yes	Yes
	Liquidity facilities—nonbank financial sector			Yes	Yes	Yes	Yes
	Liquidity facilities—business sector				Yes	Yes	Yes
	Liquidity facilities—state or local government	Yes					
	Increased limits normally available at preexisting liquidity facilities					Yes	
	Provided grace periods to repay loans from government or central bank	Yes					
	Increased maturities for liquidity facilities		Yes				Yes
01B	Reduced reserve requirements	Yes	Yes		Yes		
	Reduced liquidity requirements (e.g., liquidity coverage ratio)		Yes	Yes			
	Government securities can meet reserve and/or liquidity requirements		Yes		Yes		
	Relaxed collateral requirements for borrowing from the central bank	Yes	Yes	Yes		Yes	Yes

continued on next page

Table 14 *continued*

	Measure	Philippines	Indonesia	Thailand	Malaysia	Republic of Korea	Singapore
01C	Foreign exchange loans or swaps to domestic financial sector		Yes	Yes		Yes	Yes
	Relaxed foreign exchange reserve requirements	Yes	Yes			Yes	
	Relaxed regulatory limits to foreign exchange positions			Yes		Yes	
	Relaxed regulations on derivative positions in foreign exchange						

Source: Asian Development Bank. ADB COVID-19 Policy Database. https://covid19policy.adb.org.

(producers and suppliers). Singapore provided bridge loans to Singapore Airlines. There were a variety of approaches across countries in regard to short-term lending to different parts of the financial and nonfinancial sectors, short-term lending to subnational governments, and increasing loan maturities.

For Measure 01B, Indonesia, Malaysia, and the Philippines reduced bank reserve requirements to increase banks' abilities to lend. Both Indonesia and Malaysia further allowed banks to use government debt to meet reserve requirements against certain bank liabilities—in BI's case, banks were required to hold government securities for this purpose, while it also reduced banks' liquidity coverage ratio. The Philippines' BSP allowed some loans to SMEs to count toward meeting reserve requirements. The central banks of Indonesia, the Philippines, the ROK, Singapore, and Thailand accepted a wider range of collateral to obtain loans, both to loosen central bank credit and to encourage banks and other financial institutions to provide credit to other financial institutions and businesses.

For Measure 01C, Indonesia, the ROK, Singapore, and Thailand all provided foreign currency loans or foreign exchange swaps to the domestic financial sectors. Indonesia, the Philippines, and the ROK relaxed foreign exchange-based reserve requirements, while the ROK and Thailand relaxed regulatory limits to foreign exchange positions of financial institutions. The ROK also raised the cap on forward foreign exchange positions from 40% to 50% of capital for domestic banks and from 200% to 250% of capital for foreign-owned banks.

Table 15 examines Measure 02, which includes Measure 02A (encouraging lending to banks at a longer term than Measure 01), Measure 02B (interest rate adjustments and relaxation of regulations related to bank capital), and Measure 02C (loan guarantees). Measure 02A excludes central bank or government lending directly to nonbank financial institutions, nonfinancial businesses, households, and subnational governments (since these are in Measure 03A), but includes other lending, purchases, or collateral acceptance by the central bank or government to encourage financial institutions to offer longer-term loans to these entities. Of the six countries, only the ROK, Singapore,

Table 15. Comparison of Measure 02 for the Philippines, Indonesia, Thailand, Malaysia, the Republic of Korea, and Singapore, as of 18 December 2020

	Measure	Philippines	Indonesia	Thailand	Malaysia	Republic of Korea	Singapore
02A	Soft loans, loan purchases, or bank loans as collateral for lending to businesses			Yes			Yes
	Corporate bond purchases					Yes	
02B1	Policy rate cuts	From 3.75% to 2%	From 5% to 3.75%	From 1.25% to 0.5%	From 2.75% to 1.75%	From 1.25% to 0.5%	From 1.25% to 0%
	Other private loan rate cuts or caps	Yes		Yes	Yes		
02B2	Relaxed reporting requirements (e.g., compliance, mark-to-market, etc.)	Yes	Yes	Yes	Yes	Yes	
	Reduced banks' contributions for government insurance of liabilities			Yes			
	Relaxed loan loss oversight or provisions	Yes		Yes			Yes
	Relaxed credit standards (e.g., loan-to-value, restructuring)	Yes	Yes	Yes	Yes		
	Relaxed capital requirements	Yes		Yes			Yes
	Restricted bank dividends or buybacks			Yes			Yes
	Relaxed insurance company regulations	Yes					
02C	Loan guarantees for small and medium-sized enterprises	Yes	Yes	Yes	Yes	Yes	
	Loan guarantees for large businesses					Yes	

Source: Asian Development Bank. ADB COVID-19 Policy Database. https://covid19policy.adb.org.

and Thailand reported such activities. The ROK launched a corporate bond market stabilization fund. The Monetary Authority of Singapore (MAS) launched a facility that makes loans to eligible financial institutions at 0.1% that would, in turn, lend to SMEs that score well on environmental sustainability, social responsibility, and good governance practices.

Measure 02B is divided into Measure 02B1 (interest rate adjustments) and Measure 02B2 (relaxation of capital and related requirements). For Measure 02B1, all six central banks reduced their policy rates, with cumulative rate cuts ranging from a 0.75% cut for the Bank of Thailand and the Bank of Korea to a 1.75% cut for the BSP. MAS's policy rate ended up near 0%, whereas those for the Bank of Thailand and the Bank of Korea were nearly as low at 0.5%. In addition, other interest rates were cut by the Bank of Thailand (credit cards and personal loans) and BNM (interest rates charged on its own loans to SMEs through its special relief facility), while the BSP capped the interest rate on credit card loans.

As noted in the previous section, all six countries provided substantial relaxation of capital requirements in Measure 02B2. These included relaxing reporting requirements (all countries except Singapore), allowing financial institutions to relax credit standards either for loans or to encourage restructuring of existing loans for borrowers experiencing financial difficulties (Indonesia, Malaysia, the Philippines, and Thailand), relaxing loan loss provision requirements (the Philippines, Singapore, and Thailand), and outright reductions in capital requirements (the Philippines, Singapore, and Thailand). Thailand further reduced banks' contributions for deposit insurance. Both Singapore and Thailand also restricted bank dividend payments and equity repurchases to keep banks from reducing capital for reasons outside of loan defaults and reductions in the value of assets.

As in the previous discussion in section IV.A, loan guarantees provided to the respective financial sectors were significant in the packages of all countries except Singapore, which did not report loan guarantees. The five countries' loan guarantees were mostly for loans to SMEs, while the ROK also reported loan guarantees as part of the financial aid package for its auto industry.

Measure 03, discussed in Table 16, is composed of longer-term direct lending (or primary market bond purchases) to the private sector and state or local governments by the government, agencies of or related to the government, or the central bank (Measure 03A) and forbearances (Measure 03B). For Measure 03A, all countries except Indonesia reported longer-term direct loans to SMEs. In late April 2020, the ROK augmented its purchases of commercial paper (Measure 01A) and corporate bonds (Measure 02A) by funding a special purpose vehicle to continue these purchases. Indonesia and the Philippines reported lending to subnational governments.

Table 16. Comparison of Measure 03 for the Philippines, Indonesia, Thailand, Malaysia, the Republic of Korea, and Singapore, as of 18 December 2020

	Measure	Philippines	Indonesia	Thailand	Malaysia	Republic of Korea	Singapore
03A	Direct loans to small and medium-sized enterprises	Yes		Yes	Yes	Yes	Yes
	Direct loans to microenterprises	Yes			Yes		
	Direct loans to large corporations			Yes			Yes
	Direct loans to state or local governments	Yes	Yes				
03B	Grace periods, deferments, or moratoria for household loans and/or payments	Yes			Yes		Yes
	Grace periods, deferments, or moratoria for business loans and/or payments	Yes		Yes	Yes		Yes
	Loan or rent cancellations for households						Yes
	Loan or rent cancellations for businesses						Yes

Source: Asian Development Bank. ADB COVID-19 Policy Database. https://covid19policy.adb.org.

C.   Comparing Central Bank Support of Government Debt Markets

Table 17 presents in US dollars per capita and as a percentage of GDP the support provided by the six central banks for their respective government debt markets.

Table 17. Comparison of Measure 07 for the Philippines, Indonesia, Thailand, Malaysia, the Republic of Korea, and Singapore, as of 18 December 2020

Measure	Philippines	Indonesia	Thailand	Malaysia	Republic of Korea	Singapore
07A Direct loans and/or primary market purchases	8.3%	3.9%	0%	0%	0%	10.4%
	$283	$151	$0	$0	$0	$6,436
07B Secondary market purchases	0.3%	1.0%	0.6%	0.6%	0.2%	0%
	$11	$40	$45	$70	$48	$0

Note: Each cell reports the measures both as a percentage of gross domestic product and in terms of United States dollars per capita.
Source: Asian Development Bank. ADB COVID-19 Policy Database. https://covid19policy.adb.org.

Measure 07A is central banks' direct support of government via primary market purchases of government securities, direct loans, or national reserve drawdown, which, from Table 17, was carried out by the BSP, BI, and MAS. In Indonesia, Law No.2/2020 allowed the government to extend the state budget deficit beyond the normal limit of 3% of GDP to respond to the COVID-19 crisis, while Law No.1/2020 allowed BI to provide direct support for the government. In the Philippines, while the BSP was already allowed to provide government support, the passage of Bayanihan II in September 2020 increased the short-term advances that BSP can provide to the government, from 20% of average government revenue in the past 3 years to up to 30%. The figures for Singapore's MAS represent the government's drawdown of national reserves to finance budgetary actions related to COVID-19. (Chapter VI provides more detail on central bank support of government debt markets, particularly by the BSP and MAS, including why a drawdown belongs in Measure 07A.)

The central banks of the Philippines, Indonesia, Thailand, Malaysia, and the ROK announced secondary market purchases of government debt. Though not announced—and thus not entered in the ADB database—BNM did engage in significant purchases of government liabilities, which is reported for Measure 07B in Table 17. Secondary market operations in each case were on a modest scale compared to those carried out by the Federal Reserve, the Bank of Japan, or the Bank of Canada, for instance, with none of the five central banks in Table 17 purchasing more than 1% of its country's GDP.

It is worth recalling two additional policies that contributed to demand in government debt markets, which was noted in section IV.A. In Indonesia, BI raised the liquidity buffer ratio by 2 percentage points for conventional banks and 0.5 percentage points for Islamic banks; this additional liquidity requirement can only be met by holding government bonds purchased in the primary market. BNM likewise enabled government bonds to satisfy liquidity requirements, but in this case, government bond holdings were added to the assets that banks can normally hold to meet the requirement.

D.   Conclusions

In-depth consideration and comparison of packages across the six countries show interesting differences and similarities. The packages of the Philippines and Indonesia appear similar in terms of their monetary values, and a deeper look confirms this. The packages of Thailand and Malaysia, on the other hand, are more similar than they appear, at least as a percentage of GDP and on a per capita basis. The packages of the ROK and Singapore are much larger than the others on a per capita basis, with Singapore's package three times the size of the ROK's. As a share of GDP, however, Thailand's package (16%) is slightly larger than the ROK's (15%), while Malaysia's package (22.7%) is even closer in size to Singapore's (22.5%). The distributions across the five measures varies significantly, too, with the ROK's health and income support (Measure 05) as a percentage of GDP closer in size to that of Indonesia and the Philippines, and significantly smaller than that of Malaysia, Thailand, and especially Singapore.

Beyond the announced or reported monetary values of the measures themselves, the respective governments and central banks put forth numerous regulation and policy changes to improve liquidity, encourage private sector lending, reduce debt and payment burdens, and provide direct credit to the private sector. The analysis here suggests that there may not be an absolutely correct way to report actions that do not have obvious monetary values such as liquidity requirements, capital requirements, and forbearances. However these actions are labeled, the database's taxonomy recognizes inherently that governments and central banks nevertheless take onto their own financial statements the costs and/or the financial and macroeconomic risks of loosened financial regulations and of requirements that creditors and others provide deferred payments and restructuring options.

Finally, central banks in all six countries provided support to national governments to finance the additional costs of responding to COVID-19. Central banks in Indonesia, the Philippines, and Singapore, in particular, carried out large primary market purchases of government debt or drew down national reserves, which will be discussed in detail in Chapter VI of this report.

Chapter V

A Statistical Analysis of the Size of the Packages

Chapters III and IV discussed and analyzed the size of the COVID-19 response packages (including changes over time) that were announced and/or implemented by ADB member economies. They also provided details about the composition of the packages. ADB's developing members allocated the largest share of their packages to health and income support (Measure 05), while other ADB members allocated the largest share to credit creation (Measure 02). All member economies devoted the smallest share of their packages to equity support (Measure 04).

This chapter undertakes a statistical analysis to understand why packages differ in size across economies (section V.A). Based on this analysis, it will compare actual and expected packages per capita, as well as discuss whether the packages are adequate in responding to the COVID-19 crisis (section V.B).

A.   Why Do Packages Differ in Size?

To measure size, the analysis uses two proxies: package per capita and package as a percentage of GDP. The analysis is undertaken at the level of the total for Measures 01–04 and Measure 05. Table 18 presents the data sources and descriptive statistics of the variables used in the analysis, including variables that may be correlated with the size of the packages, using 18 December 2020 data.

Table 18. Size of the Packages and Correlates, Descriptive Statistics, as of 18 December 2020

Size of the Packages	Data Sources	Mean	Std Dev	Min	Max
Total package per capita ($)[a]	ADB COVID-19 Policy Database, World Bank WDI, ADB ADO Database, CEIC	5,592	8,676	0.2 Turkmenistan	29,046 Luxembourg
Total package (% of GDP)[a]	ADB COVID-19 Policy Database, IMF WEO Database, ADB ADO Database, CEIC	15.8	14.9	0.002 Turkmenistan	66.1 Japan
Measure 05 per capita ($)[a]	ADB COVID-19 Policy Database, World Bank WDI, ADB ADO Database, CEIC	2,331	3,797	0[b]	17,967 Japan
Measure 05 (% of GDP)[a]	ADB COVID-19 Policy Database, IMF WEO Database, ADB ADO Database, CEIC	7.5	7.1	0[b]	43.6 Japan
Sum of Measures 01–04 per capita ($)[a]	ADB COVID-19 Policy Database, World Bank WDI, ADB ADO Database, CEIC	3,050	5,371	0[c]	20,638 Finland
Sum of Measures 01–04 (% of GDP)[a]	ADB COVID-19 Policy Database, IMF WEO Database, ADB ADO Database, CEIC	7.4	10.3	0[c]	43.0 Finland
Correlates					
GDP per capita 2019 ($)[a]	IMF WEO Database, World Bank WDI, ADB ADO Database, CEIC	22,604	25,757	492 Afghanistan	112,040 Luxembourg
COVID-19 cases per 100,000 population as of 18 Dec 2020[a]	ECDC, Center for Systems Science and Engineering at Johns Hopkins University, Worldometer, World Bank WDI, ADB ADO Database, and CEIC	1,203	1,765	0[d]	7,104 Luxembourg
Population of at least 65 years old (% of total population in 2019)	World Bank WDI	11.0	6.9	2.6 Afghanistan	28.0 Japan
Wage and salaried workers (% of total employment in 2019)	World Bank WDI	64.2	23.8	17.7 Afghanistan	93.8 United States
Self-employed (% of total employment in 2019)	World Bank WDI	35.8	23.8	6.2 United States	82.3 Afghanistan
Vulnerable employment (% of total employment in 2019)	World Bank WDI	32.8	24.5	3.8 United States	80.1 Lao PDR
Total stock of debt liabilities issued by the central government (% of GDP)	IMF Global Debt Database	51.2	36.9	2.6 Brunei Darussalam	198.4 Japan

ADB = Asian Development Bank, ADO = Asian Development Outlook, COVID-19 = coronavirus disease, ECDC = European Centre for Disease Prevention and Control, GDP = gross domestic product, IMF = International Monetary Fund, Lao PDR = Lao People's Democratic Republic, OECD = Organisation for Economic Co-operation and Development, WDI = World Development Indicators, WEO = World Economic Outlook.

[a] Data calculated based on the listed sources.
[b] Brunei Darussalam, Nepal, and Turkmenistan.
[c] Afghanistan, Bhutan, Cambodia, the Federated States of Micronesia, Kiribati, the Marshall Islands, Nauru, Palau, Samoa, Solomon Islands, Tajikistan, Tonga, Turkmenistan, Tuvalu, and Uzbekistan.
[d] The Cook Islands, the Federated States of Micronesia, Kiribati, Nauru, Niue, Palau, Tonga, Turkmenistan, and Tuvalu.

Source: Authors' compilation and calculations.

The following observations are based on the summary measures in Table 18:

(i)   The largest package per capita belongs to Luxembourg ($29,406), while the smallest belongs to Turkmenistan. Nineteen economies in the ADB COVID-19 Policy Database have a package per capita that is above the mean ($5,592). In addition, package per capita is at most $500 in 29 economies; at most $10,000 in 52 economies; and at least $22,000 in eight economies. Hong Kong, China is the only ADB developing member in the top eight of package per capita. Figure 4 illustrates the distribution of these packages.

Figure 4. Number of Economies by Package per Capita, as of 18 December 2020

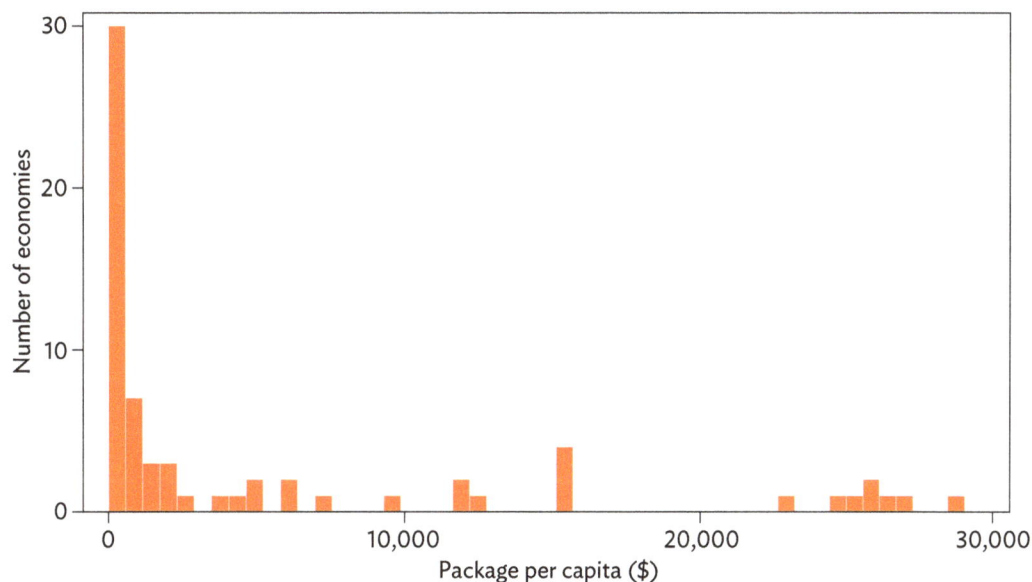

Source: Authors' calculations. See data sources in Table 18.

(ii)   As a percentage of GDP, Japan has the largest package, while Turkmenistan still has the smallest. The packages of 50 ADB member economies are at most 20% of their GDP, and the packages of five member economies are at least 50% of their GDP.

(iii)   The largest amounts of Measure 05, both per capita and as a percentage of GDP, belong to Japan. For Measures 01–04, Finland has the largest amounts per capita and as a percentage of GDP. Hong Kong, China is the only ADB developing member in the top 10 of amounts allocated to Measures 01–04.

(iv)   Nine ADB developing members (the Cook Islands, the Federated States of Micronesia, Kiribati, Nauru, Niue, Palau, Tonga, Turkmenistan, and Tuvalu) had no confirmed COVID-19 cases as of 18 December 2020.

(v)   Japan has the highest percentage of people at least 65 years old, while Afghanistan has the lowest percentage.

(vi) The US has the highest percentage of salaried workers in total employment, while the Lao People's Democratic Republic has the highest percentage of vulnerable employment in total employment.

Figure 5 shows the relationship between package per capita and the correlates listed in Table 18.

The estimated equations in Table 19 show log-log ordinary least squares regressions (with robust standard errors) of total package per capita against its correlates.[22] These regressions do not contain regional fixed effects (dummies for the five ADB regions) because these were insignificant in many cases. The analysis only shows the regressions that produced some meaningful and statistically significant results. Most of the right-hand-side variables are highly correlated and, consequently, results are very poor when they are together in a regression.

Table 19. Package per Capita (log) and Its Correlates (log), as of 18 December 2020

Equation	Regression Model	R^2
(1)	Package per capita = –7.68*** + 1.56 x GDP per capita***	0.707
(1a)	Package per capita = –5.74*** + 1.38 x GDP per capita***	0.883
(2)	Package per capita = –7.38*** + 1.49 x GDP per capita*** + 0.07 x Cases per 100,000 population (NS)	0.713
(3)	Package per capita = –6.04*** + 1.06 x GDP per capita*** + 1.35 x Population of at least 65 years old as a percentage of total population**	0.741
(4)	Package per capita = –3.12 (NS) + 3.06 x Population of at least 65 years old as a percentage of total population*** + 0.74 x Wage and salaried workers as a percentage of total employment (NS)	0.669
(5)	Package per capita = 4.25 (NS) + 2.57 x Population of at least 65 years old as a percentage of total population*** – 0.98 x Self-employed as a percentage of total employment**	0.692
(6)	Package per capita = 4.04* + 2.47 x Population of at least 65 years old as a percentage of total population*** – 0.90 x Vulnerable employment as a percentage of total employment***	0.697
(7)	Package per capita = –8.06*** + 1.50 x GDP per capita*** + 0.25 x Total stock of debt liabilities issued by the central government as a percentage of GDP (NS)	0.698

GDP = gross domestic product, NS = not significant.

Notes: The study tested for the presence of heteroskedasticity using the Breusch–Pagan test and rejected the null hypothesis (no heteroskedasticity) in equations (1)–(7). Equation (1): All regional fixed effects (FE) are insignificant. Equation (2): East Asia and Central and West Asia are the only significant regional FE. Equation (3): All regional FE are insignificant. Equation (4): Central and West Asia is the only significant regional FE. Equations (5) and (6): East Asia is the only significant regional FE. Equation (7): All regional FE are insignificant. ***, **, and * denote statistical significance at the 1%, 5%, and 10% level, respectively.

Source: Authors' estimates.

---

[22] Though the ADB COVID-19 Policy Database provides information biweekly from 20 April to 18 December 2020, these data cannot be pooled as the right-hand-side variables do not change. The study has run the regressions for each version and the results are qualitatively very similar.

Figure 5. Package per Capita and Correlates, as of 18 December 2020

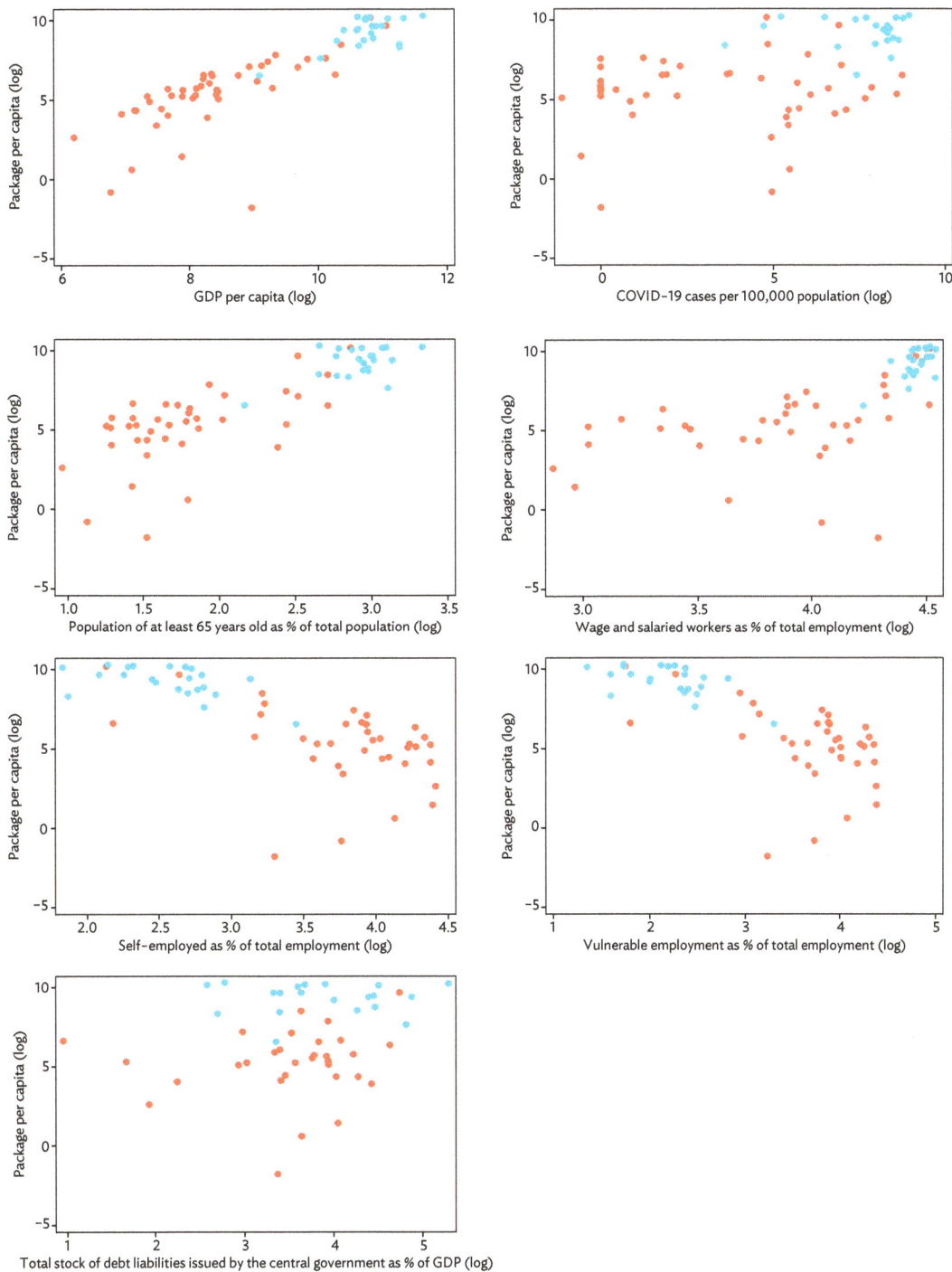

ADB = Asian Development Bank, COVID-19 = coronavirus disease, GDP = gross domestic product.
Note: ADB's developing members are in red. Other ADB members are in blue.
Source: Authors' calculations.

Equation (1) indicates that the elasticity of package per capita with respect to income per capita is 1.56. The log of income per capita alone explains 71% of the variation in the log of package per capita. Naturally, this regression is equivalent to regressing total package on GDP (positive coefficient) and population (negative coefficient). This high elasticity indicates that the intended total packages increase much more than proportionally with income per capita. It is clear that rich economies have dedicated significantly more resources to combat COVID-19 than developing economies.

The analysis also estimated five other regressands against income per capita (not shown in Table 19). A similar result was obtained when the package refers to only Measure 05. Indeed, the elasticity of Measure 05 per capita with respect to income per capita is still very high at 1.51. The results when the dependent variable is the total package as a percentage of GDP or Measure 05 as a percentage of GDP are also statistically significant, but the elasticities are much lower at 0.56 and 0.51, respectively. The corresponding elasticities for the sum of Measures 01–04 per capita and as a percentage of GDP are larger than the previous ones, at 1.94 and 0.62, respectively.

Figure 6 plots the regression line corresponding to equation (1). Only a few economies exhibit a substantial deviation from the line. These are the Lao People's Democratic Republic, Myanmar, Tajikistan, and Turkmenistan. For this reason, equation (1) was reestimated without these four countries in equation (1a).

Figure 6. Package per Capita and Gross Domestic Product per Capita: Regression Line

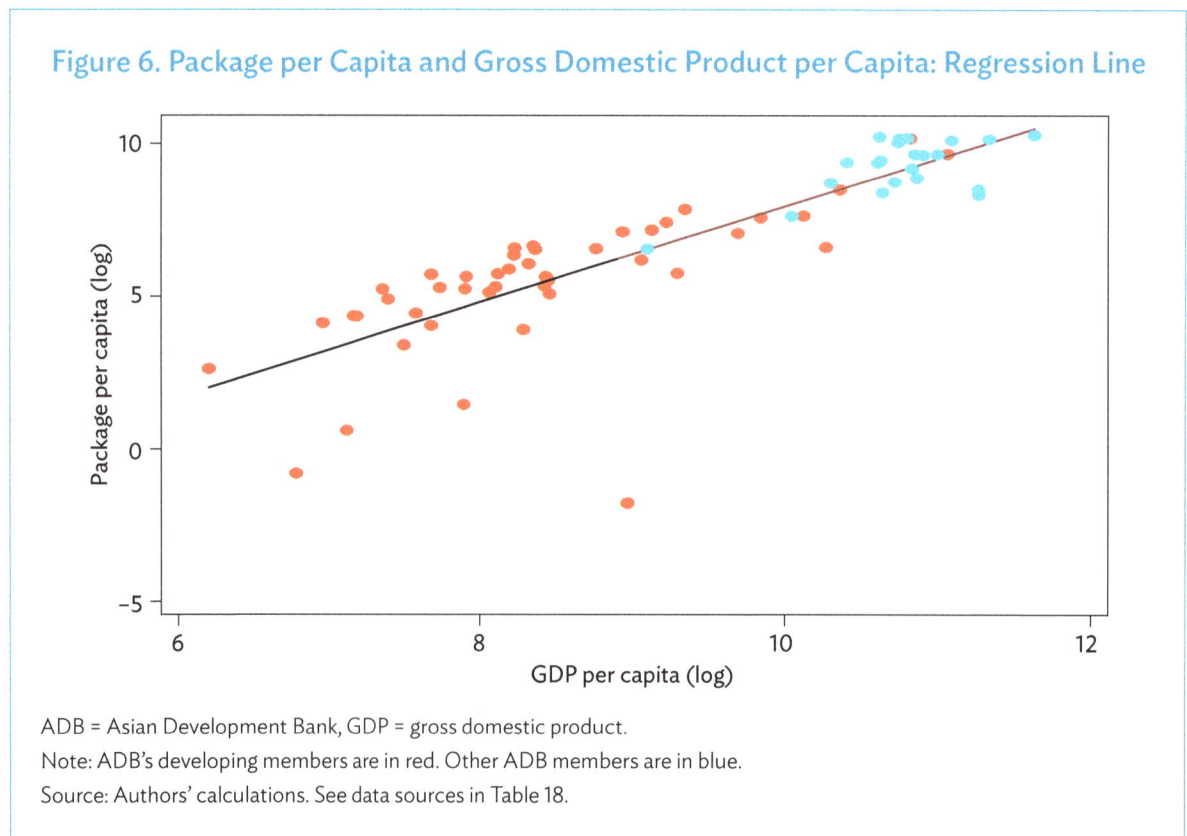

ADB = Asian Development Bank, GDP = gross domestic product.

Note: ADB's developing members are in red. Other ADB members are in blue.

Source: Authors' calculations. See data sources in Table 18.

The elasticity of package per capita in equation (1a) is still high at 1.38, and the R-squared of the regression increases to 88%. One can only speculate about why these four countries have spent much less than what their GDP per capita indicates. One possibility is that there are still concepts and/or amounts that the ADB COVID-19 Policy Database has not properly accounted for.

Equations (2) and (3) show regressions of package per capita (log) against income per capita (log), controlling for the number of COVID-19 cases per 100,000 (log) and the share of the population at least 65 years old (log), respectively. The number of COVID-19 cases per 100,000 is not a significant determinant of package per capita, while the percentage of the population at least 65 years old is a positive determinant (this percentage is higher in high-income economies). In this latter regression, the coefficient of GDP per capita becomes about 1 and is compensated by the coefficient of the percentage of population at least 65 years old, which is 1.35.

Equations (4)–(6) show regressions of package per capita (log) against the percentage of the population at least 65 years old (log), wage and salaried workers as a percentage of total employment (log), self-employed as a percentage of total employment (log), and vulnerable employment as a percentage of total employment (log). As expected, package per capita decreases with the percentage of self-employed in total employment and the percentage of vulnerable employment in total employment. These two variables decrease as economies get richer. On the other hand, wage and salaried workers as a percentage of total employment is not statistically related to package per capita. The elasticity of the percentage of population at least 65 years old is very high at 2.5–3. This share is also much higher in advanced economies.

Finally, equation (7) shows that package per capita is not statistically related to the stock of central government debt as a percentage of GDP.

B.   Are the Packages Adequate to Address the COVID-19 Pandemic?

Based on the results discussed in section V.A, Table 20 shows actual and expected packages per capita, where the latter are derived from equations (1), (3), (5), and (6) above. The expected packages per capita are (subjectively) classified as "close" to the actual package per capita if the expected amounts are within ±10% of the actual package per capita. These are the cells without any color. Gold cells show expected packages per capita that are above 10% of the actual package per capita, and green cells show expected packages per capita that are below 10% of the actual package.

Table 20. Actual and Expected Package per Capita, as of 18 December 2020

	Actual Package per Capita ($)	Expected Package per Capita ($)			
		Eq (1)	Eq (3)	Eq (5)	Eq (6)
ADB's developing members					
Afghanistan	14	7	6	11	12
Armenia	207	239	486	1,001	874
Azerbaijan	159	252	231	134	153
Bangladesh	85	64	67	87	89
Bhutan	564	175	167	111	105
Brunei Darussalam	734	4,268	1,178	576	662
Cambodia	134	48	49	81	77
Cook Islands	1,934	2,197	–	–	–
Federated States of Micronesia	308	148	90	–	–
Fiji	699	409	267	144	136
Georgia	681	218	659	1,578	1,376
Hong Kong, China	25,898	10,037	10,837	13,585	13,782
India	302	74	99	117	114
Indonesia	426	204	184	150	149
Kazakhstan	1,285	719	593	567	510
Kiribati	187	45	39	–	–
Kyrgyz Republic	77	33	37	107	103
Lao People's Democratic Republic	4	104	70	37	37
Malaysia	2,528	1,011	651	427	420
Maldives	316	937	260	87	95
Marshall Islands	714	176	–	–	–
Mongolia	768	214	115	61	59
Myanmar	2	31	50	123	121
Nauru	483	646	–	–	–
Nepal	61	24	40	87	85
Pakistan	77	34	35	57	57
Palau	1,162	1,735	–	–	–
Papua New Guinea	187	105	56	24	25
People's Republic of China	1,658	835	1,134	855	755
Philippines	200	145	122	151	152
Republic of Korea	4,799	4,928	5,461	3,198	3,225
Samoa	281	243	157	137	137
Singapore	15,629	14,769	8,829	3,401	3,671
Solomon Islands	56	74	46	31	32
Sri Lanka	49	193	390	820	752

continued on next page

Table 20 *continued*

	Actual Package per Capita ($)	Expected Package per Capita ($)			
		Eq (1)	Eq (3)	Eq (5)	Eq (6)
Taipei,China	2,053	3,396	–	–	–
Tajikistan	0.44	18	14	32	32
Thailand	1,208	534	931	957	863
Timor-Leste	196	81	61	47	47
Tonga	250	249	205	138	131
Turkmenistan	0.17	562	251	139	134
Tuvalu	360	167	–	–	–
Uzbekistan	30	56	53	87	85
Vanuatu	167	136	70	29	30
Viet Nam	280	107	160	244	230
Other ADB members					
Australia	15,113	11,519	10,470	5,558	6,247
Austria	9,696	10,276	12,376	12,083	13,542
Belgium	6,199	8,620	10,932	10,256	10,047
Canada	22,699	8,914	10,115	7,761	8,014
Denmark	15,373	13,363	15,729	20,020	21,937
Finland	26,236	9,775	14,636	16,106	15,463
France	11,678	7,256	10,698	14,693	15,879
Germany	25,624	9,042	13,395	19,998	23,422
Ireland	4,870	20,271	13,185	4,568	4,740
Italy	11,792	5,291	10,171	10,309	10,229
Japan	27,199	7,384	16,629	37,781	31,381
Luxembourg	29,046	35,771	19,474	7,966	8,480
Netherlands	7,030	10,798	13,282	9,363	8,925
New Zealand	4,406	7,612	7,956	5,115	5,630
Norway	4,042	20,349	17,194	17,095	15,318
Portugal	2,015	3,017	6,683	13,090	13,088
Spain	5,994	4,490	7,348	9,822	10,192
Sweden	15,384	10,593	13,650	17,385	18,620
Switzerland	25,213	22,562	20,738	9,560	11,055
Turkey	693	685	685	623	613
United Kingdom	12,578	7,449	9,552	8,900	7,559
United States	24,559	15,392	13,057	15,076	16,339

– = not available, ADB = Asian Development Bank.

Notes: Cells in orange indicate that the expected package per capita is higher than the actual package per capita. Cells in blue indicate that the expected package per capita is lower than the actual package per capita. A cell without color means that the expected package per capita is close to the actual package per capita. There is no data for Niue on actual package per capita.

Source: Authors' calculations based on regression equations (1), (3), (5), and (6) in Table 19. See data sources in Table 18.

This information can be used to discuss the normative question: is a package on a per capita basis adequate to address the COVID-19 pandemic? This is a difficult question with no easy answer, as it depends on the government's objectives, both with respect to the pandemic and other economic objectives (e.g., fear of running a fiscal deficit), and how it perceives the situation. Since there are four models, the results are often not very clear and so the conclusions require some judgment. Take, for example, the case of Singapore. Its actual package per capita is right in line with its income per capita, but it is much larger than what it should be given the percentage of the total population at least 65 years old, wage and salaried workers as a percentage of total employment, self-employed as a percentage of total employment, and vulnerable employment as a percentage of total employment.

If we look at ADB's developing members, we see large countries such as India or Indonesia with seemingly small packages per capita ($302 and $426, respectively), but still larger than what they should be given the study's control variables. The PRC's package ($1,658 per capita) is larger than the packages of these two countries and well over the values predicted by the regressions. This is also the case of Malaysia and Thailand, which have actual packages of $2,528 and $1,208 per capita, respectively. On the other hand, the actual package of the Philippines, despite being larger than the predicted values, is smaller in absolute value ($200 per capita) than the packages of other ADB member economies. Increasing this package to about $300 per capita would imply a total package that is 50% larger, about $32 billion as opposed to $22 billion. Pakistan's package at $77 per capita is also relatively small. Increasing its package to $100 per capita would imply an increase in the country's total package from $17 billion to about $22 billion.

The predicted package per capita of Luxembourg (despite having the highest actual package per capita) is above the actual value given the country's income per capita. Portugal's package ranks second to lowest among other ADB members. It appears to be small according to all models. This is also the case for the packages of Belgium, the Netherlands, New Zealand, and Norway. On the other hand, the actual packages of Australia, Canada, Finland, Italy, Switzerland, the UK, and the US are higher than what their respective models predict.

C.   Conclusions

Income per capita is a very good predictor of package per capita. Other significant predictors are the share of the population at least 65 years old, the share of self-employment in total employment, and the share of vulnerable employment in total employment. The study finds that rich economies have spent very significant amounts to contain COVID-19, often above what the models predict. Indeed, taking a look at Table 20, it appears that the actual package is above the expected package in many cases.

Chapter VI

How "Monetization" Really Works—Examples from Countries' Policy Responses to COVID-19

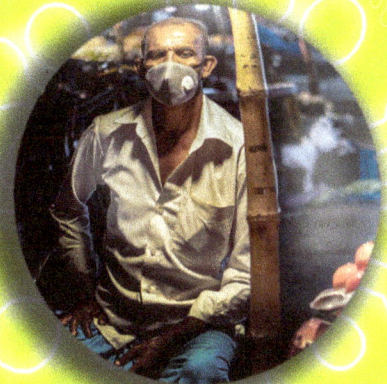

The severe economic downturn caused by the COVID-19 pandemic has forced governments worldwide to increase spending even as tax revenues simultaneously collapsed. As discussed in Chapter III, ADB's 68 members plus the ECB and the EU have announced packages worth over $27 trillion as of 18 December 2020, according to the ADB COVID-19 Policy Database. Of this amount, $3.6 trillion corresponds to packages by ADB's 46 developing members. Almost $9 trillion have been allocated to directly support incomes (spending, tax cuts, etc.), of which $1.8 trillion is from ADB's developing members.

Central banks in several of these economies are financing a significant share of this direct income support through direct lending or purchases of government bonds in primary and/or secondary markets. According to the ADB COVID-19 Policy Database, central bank financial support of government across all ADB members has reached around $3.5 trillion, plus nearly $400 billion more from the ECB. This accounts for over 35% of the direct income support governments have authorized. Among ADB's developing members, central banks contributed only about $132 billion or around 7% of the developing members' direct income support. In some countries, however, the central bank's support of the government is a large share of the government's direct income support. For instance, announced support for the governments of Indonesia and the Philippines by their respective central banks is well over 100% of each government's direct income support to the private sector.

Of course, with the central bank's financial support of government, there is always controversy about the potential for inflation and/or the threat of fiscal dominance. Less often understood is that governments and their central banks are already carrying out operations daily that are inherently interdependent. These operations provide the necessary context for thinking carefully about how central bank's financial support of government is occurring now and for helping clarify where more or less concern is appropriate. In particular, whereas standard thinking has been that central bank support of government deficits amounts to "printing money" and/or "monetizing government debt," actual operations and accounting show this is not the case. Instead, these operations simply replace an interest-earning government liability with an interest-earning central bank liability, though they obviously also can enable more central bank influence over risk-free interest rates in the domestic currency.

The purpose of this chapter is to describe monetization through operations and accounting, within the context of the experiences of three countries—the Philippines, Singapore, and the PRC—during the first half of 2020 in response to COVID-19. Section VI.A presents three core points for understanding monetization through the operations and accounting of real world central banks, which serves as a reminder that both the view that the interest rate is determined within the context of government deficits in a loanable funds market and standard, simplistic views of printing money long prevalent among economists and policy makers are completely at odds with reality. Sections VI.B, VI.C, and VI.D, which cover the Philippines, Singapore, and the PRC, respectively, examine a significant part of the countries' response to COVID-19 relevant to monetization. In the end, consistent with the use of quotes around "monetization" in the title of this chapter, it is not what most think it is. Instead, it is not nearly as dangerous as its critics argue, but also not necessarily as useful as its supporters claim or hope. And, without most even knowing it, it is already happening, even in normal times.

A.   Central Bank Operations and Government Debt

Table 21 lists countries (plus the ECB) whose central banks are known to have engaged in some form of support of government debt, separated into those that have engaged in direct lending and/or primary market purchases of government debt,[23] secondary market purchases,[24] and/or secondary market purchases for directly setting rates on government debt along the yield curve, either outright or in exchange for sales of short-term government bills (maturity swaps, denoted by superscript "a" in the table). Some countries appear in multiple columns: Indonesia, New Zealand, the Philippines, and the UK are in columns 1 and 2, and India in columns 1 and 3.

There are three core points to understand how central bank operations support governments. First, central banks set interest rate targets or target ranges, which is necessary because of the flexibility in the quantity of central bank reserve balances (RBs) required on a daily basis to ensure a smooth functioning of the payments system and stability in wholesale funding markets. RBs are central bank liabilities that banks use to settle payments and, where applicable, meet regulatory requirements for liquid balances against their own liabilities. Central banks thus carry out daily operations using a version of either a corridor system or a floor system to achieve their interest rate target, both of which appear in Figure 7.

In the corridor system, the central bank's penalty rate for borrowing from its standing facility and the rate paid on RBs (interest on reserves [IOR], or zero for a central bank that does not pay IOR) together set a corridor for the market interest rate to fluctuate within. The central bank then adds or drains RBs via open market operations, loans, and so on, to shift the vertical portion of the supply of RBs (SRB) as it accommodates shifts in banks' demand for RBs (DRB) at the central bank's interest rate target (i^*), or to offset changes to its own balance sheet that would otherwise alter the quantity of RBs and move the market rate away from i^*. In a floor system, the central bank simply ensures the SRB is shifted right to well beyond any projected downward-sloping portion of DRB. From basic supply and

---

[23] This is exclusive of some central banks' normal practice of rolling over their maturing holdings of government debt in primary markets.

[24] This is exclusive of, or in addition to, the normal practice of many central banks that already regularly purchase government debt in secondary markets in order to replenish banks' reserve balances debited as banks' purchase of physical currency for their customers' withdrawals.

Table 21. Countries that Received Support from Their Central Banks in Response to COVID-19

Direct Loans or Primary Market Purchases (1)	Secondary Market Purchases (2)	Secondary Market Purchases: Yield Curve Control or Maturity Swap (3)
Canada	Bangladesh	Australia
India	Canada	Japan
Indonesia	Euro area	India[a]
New Zealand	Fiji	Mexico[a]
Philippines	Indonesia	
United Kingdom	Malaysia	
	New Zealand	
	Papua New Guinea	
	Philippines	
	Republic of Korea	
	Solomon Islands	
	South Africa	
	Sweden	
	Thailand	
	Turkey	
	United Kingdom	
	United States	

COVID-19 = coronavirus disease.

[a] Countries engaged in maturity swaps.

Source: Authors' compilation based on ADB COVID-19 Policy Database at https://covid19policy.adb.org.

Figure 7. Corridor and Floor Systems for Central Bank Interest Rate Targeting

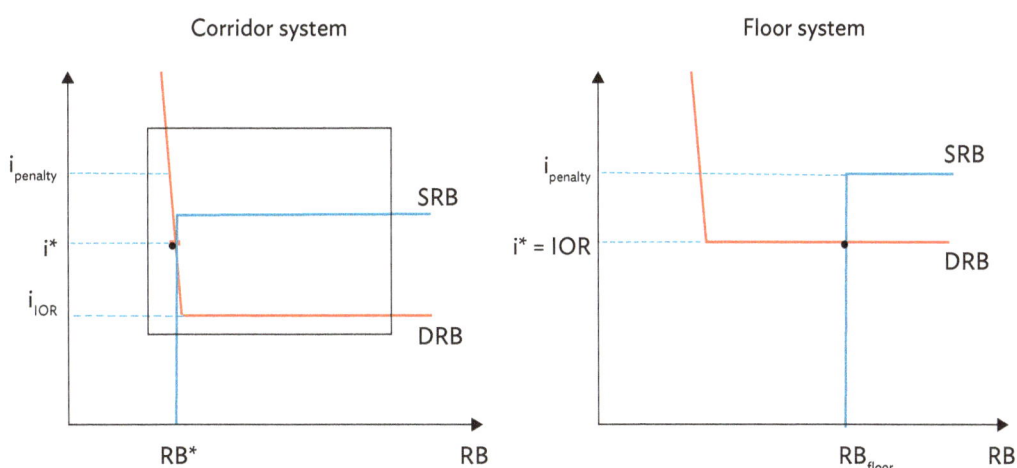

DRB = demand for RBs, i^* = interest rate target, $i_{penalty}$ = penalty rate, IOR = interest on reserves, RB = reserve balance, SRB = supply of RBs.

Source: Authors.

demand analysis, this pushes the price (the market interest rate) to zero. If the central bank wants to set its interest rate target above zero it must pay IOR equal to i*. Thus, the floor in the floor system is either zero or the IOR, which becomes the de facto interest rate target. The quantity of RBs in the corridor system graph is an equilibrium (RB*), while any quantity of RBs along the horizontal portion of DRB achieves the target rate in the floor system.

The second core point is that government spending, tax revenues, and bond sales in the domestic currency all occur on the central bank's balance sheet because the government's account is a liability of the central bank. From simple double-entry accounting (T-accounts), the financial flows into and out of the government's account will have the opposite effect on the quantity of RBs circulating. Table 22 shows the T-account entries for a government deficit and a government bond sale, respectively. Considering Table 22 and Figure 7 together, the deficit raises RBs, placing downward pressure on the market rate in the corridor system, though obviously not in the floor system given the floor's presence at IOR = i*. The bond sale drains RBs and offsets the deficit's effect on the quantity of RBs in both systems; in the corridor system, the pressure on the market rate to fall is reversed, while as long as the quantity of RBs in the floor system remains to the right of the downward-sloping portion of DRB throughout, there is no effect on the market interest rate.

Table 22. T-Accounts for Government Deficit and Bond Sale

	Government		Central Bank		Banks		Dealers		Households	
	A	L/E	A	L/E	A	L/E	A	L/E	A	L/E
Government deficit	Acct @ CB (−)	Net Worth (−)		RBs (+) Govt Acct (−)	RBs (+)	HH Dep (+)			Dep (+)	Net Worth (+)
Government bond sale	Acct @ CB (+)	Bonds (+)		RBs (−) Govt Acct (+)	RBs (−)	Dealer Dep (−)	Dep (−) Bonds (+)			

A = assets, Acct @ CB = the government's account at the central bank on the government's assets, Dep = deposits, Govt Acct = the government's account at the central bank on the central bank's liabilities, HH = household, L/E = liabilities and equity, Net Worth = assets minus liabilities, RB = reserve balance.
Source: Authors.

Even in normal times, the flows to and from the government due to spending, revenues, and bond sales are not perfectly timed. In the US, for instance, prior to the 2008 GFC, the US Treasury would transfer from or to its account at the Federal Reserve to or from accounts it held at thousands of private banks to offset this lack of daily synchronization and its effect on the quantity of RBs, thus largely allowing the Federal Reserve to avoid having to offset these flows itself in its own operations (Kelton [Bell] 2000, Tymoigne 2014). Other countries like the PRC that use a Treasury Single Account System (TSAS) instead leave these offsetting operations to their central banks to integrate into day-to-day operations for achieving the interest rate target (e.g., He and Jia 2020). A central bank using a corridor system will have to offset these flows if they move the market rate away from the central bank's target, either by changing its assets (more or fewer loans or open market operations, for instance) or changing its own non-RB liabilities to counter the flow to and from the government's account. In a floor system, the central bank again simply ensures the quantity of RBs is "ample," such that SRB is to the right of the downward-sloping part of DRB.

The corollary here is that when central banks finance the government, whether directly (primary market or direct loans) or indirectly (secondary market), they cannot do so without sterilizing these operations. Figure 8 shows these operations in the corridor and floor systems. Both direct and indirect central bank finance shift SRB to the right. A central bank in a corridor system will need to respond by draining RBs to achieve the target rate, either by issuing its own liabilities at a rate similar to its target rate or some combination of reducing its assets via sales or allowing its claims on the private sector to mature and not roll over. In a floor system, the central bank responds by paying interest on the additional RB, which become essentially an interest-bearing overnight debt issued by the central bank earning the central bank's target rate. Thus, the central bank is not printing money because it is not operationally possible in either system.

Figure 8. Sterilizing Central Bank Support of Government in Corridor and Floor Systems

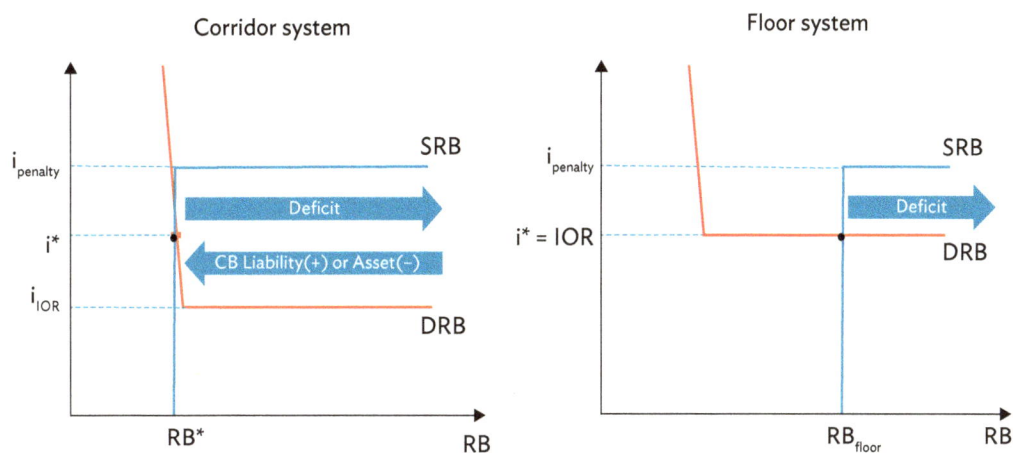

CB = central bank, DRB = demand for RBs, i* = interest rate target, $i_{penalty}$ = penalty rate, IOR = interest on reserves, RB = reserve balance, SRB = supply of RBs.
Source: Authors.

Lastly, as the central bank ends up paying interest on its own liabilities issued in these operations within a floor system, this reduction in its net income will lead to an in-kind reduction in the central bank's remittances to the government, reducing the government's own budget position such that it is effectively servicing the debt itself as if it had issued bonds. It is the standard practice across countries in which central banks remit their profits (or some percentage of profits), often legally prescribed, to the government. Remittances arise mostly from interest paid by the government to the central bank on government liabilities held by the central bank, which is in essence returned to the government. In terms of accounting, the remittance is a simple debit from the central bank's equity and credit to the government's account at the central bank. Likewise, though, if the central bank must pay interest on its liabilities issued when it acquires government debt in the secondary market or when a government incurs a deficit the central bank directly finances, the central bank's profits are reduced in kind and so are its remittances. This is important for understanding government debt operations, since it means that when the central bank acquires the government's debt in a floor system, the cost of servicing this debt is still effectively borne by the government indirectly through reduced remittances from the central bank.

The final core point relates to interest rates on domestic currency government debt—the yield curve for the risk-free rate—which is a benchmark from which markets price other financial assets. This means that interest rates on government debt are an integral part of the transmission of monetary policy. This is well known in principle, but the implications are usually not. A competitive, highly liquid market for government debt will price the yield curve mostly based on the central bank's current target rate and the market's expected path for the central bank's target rate. This is because sufficient funding liquidity (that is, the ability to finance and refinance asset positions) and market liquidity (the ability to buy or sell quickly in large quantities and at low cost) in a competitive market bring the returns from holding the government bonds in line (again, mostly) with the borrowing costs of acquiring the funds to purchase them—namely, the current central bank target rate and its expected path. Where government debt markets are highly liquid, central banks enable this via at least an implicit support for markets and financial liquidity to achieve their interest rate targets (or target ranges), especially (or necessarily) where central banks' operations occur with a network of government bond dealers.

The foregoing discussion suggests there are primarily two reasons for a central bank to support government liabilities:

(i)   to reduce the yield curve (or portions of it) below current market expectations of the path of the central bank's target rate; and

(ii)   to support market functioning where liquidity is insufficient, perhaps temporarily impaired by a systemic shock, without which monetary policy will not transmit through financial markets or will transmit perversely.

Representative examples of the first reason (i) are the yield curve control (YCC) operations of the Bank of Japan since 2016 and the Federal Reserve's quantitative easing (QE) operations during 2010–2015. The Bank of Japan's YCC operations target explicit, very low interest rates across the yield curve. The Federal Reserve's QE operations during the first half of the 2010s did this as well, but via an announced quantity of bond purchases rather than an announced desired interest rate for any particular maturity. In both cases, the central banks' operations were carried out using a floor system, and the RBs created by these operations earned interest. The two central banks have different frameworks for this, with RBs of banks earning 0.25% at the Federal Reserve and excess RBs at the Bank of Japan earning negative rates since 2016.

In the course of responding to COVID-19, at least initially, many central banks intervened to support government bond markets due to the second reason (ii) above, as the Federal Reserve did in March 2020, only 6 months after it had intervened to provide financial liquidity to government bond dealers in September 2019 and continued to support government bond markets thereafter through Treasury bill purchases.[25] This reduction in bond market liquidity happened in rich countries, such as the UK, as well as emerging market countries, such as Indonesia and the Philippines, prompting an active central bank response in these countries even beyond their response during the 2008 GFC. The actions even brought about a new term to describe them—"market functioning" operations—in order to differentiate these operations related to the second reason (ii) above from those related to the first reason (i). To be clear, neither (i) or (ii) are inherently tied to YCC, QE, or whatever other strategies central banks might pursue. Pursuing operations related to (ii), the Federal Reserve's approach was similar to earlier rounds of QE whereby it did not announce target rates across the yield curve, whereas the Reserve Bank of Australia did set a rate for the benchmark 3-year government bond.

To conclude this section, consider how different a system based on the above three core points is from the traditional view of government borrowing in a loanable funds market and central bank printing money to support government debt operations. As the three core points illustrate using basic accounting identities, the government's deficit adds to private saving rather than drains it. Because the deficit and bond sale both occur on the central bank's balance sheet, it is not the private sector's saving that finances government bond sales but rather the private sector's acquisition of the central bank's liabilities that enables it to purchase the government's bonds. Rather than government bond sales raising interest rates as implied in the loanable funds market view, the sales into a liquid bond market are backstopped by central bank support of bond dealers such that interest rates on the bonds will be mostly based on the anticipated path of the central bank's target rate. Rather than printing money and thereby adding "jet fuel" to government deficits, central bank support of government debt operations directly or in secondary markets simply leave a central bank liability that will be paid at the central bank's target rate path as a replacement of a government liability that would earn a similar rate. Ultimately, due to remittance arrangements, the government will still pay the interest. The next section further illustrates these points in the context of the Philippines during the early months of the COVID-19 pandemic response.

---

[25] See Fleming (2020), Duffie (2020), and Logan (2020) for a discussion. In the Federal Reserve's case, its own liquidity and capital regulations contributed to continuing liquidity issues, as Pozsar (2019a, 2019b) had warned earlier, that worsened in the COVID-19 crisis.

B.   The Bangko Sentral ng Pilipinas and Failed Treasury Auctions in March 2020

The government bond market in the Philippines encountered several liquidity issues in March and April 2020. In particular, the Bureau of the Treasury (BTr) experienced failed auctions throughout the second half of March (this does not mean there were no buyers; in fact, most of the auctions were almost fully subscribed, though it is not uncommon for the BTr to reject bids it deems too high). The Philippines' BSP responded with the following series of actions:

(i)   17 March: Cancelled Term Deposit Facility (TDF) auctions that drain RBs to achieve the target rate so that these would not compete with the BTr's auctions.

(ii)   23 March: Authorized a 300 billion peso (₱) repurchase agreement with the BTr with a maturity of 3 months, which the BSP could extend for 3 more months at the due date.

(iii)   24 March: Increased interventions in the secondary government bond market with a new daily 1-hour facility to buy select BTr securities.

(iv)   26 March: Remitted ₱20 billion in advance dividends to the BTr.

(v)   8 April: Increased interventions again in the secondary government bond market by making all BTr securities eligible for purchase during the new facility's hour of operation.

The action on 17 March 2020 involves the BSP's corridor system for achieving its interest rate target, as the BSP regularly issues its own term liabilities at roughly its own interest rate target to achieve its target rate in normal times.[26] The 24 March and 8 April 2020 actions show the BSP acting as a backstop to the government bond market, attempting to generate greater market liquidity. The 23 March and 26 March 2020 actions are the BSP's direct finance of the government.

The 23 March 2020 repurchase agreement was essentially a 6-month direct loan (assuming renewal after the first 3 months) from the BSP to the BTr. Table 23 walks through the operations involved in this ₱300 billion loan and their effects on the interest rate corridor targeting system for this loan and its eventual repayment. The first transaction is simply the BSP crediting the BTr's account. In transaction 2, the BTr incurs a deficit and RBs rise. To achieve its target interest rate, the BSP would have to return to TDF auctions to drain any RBs that would otherwise push the market rate below its target rate (transaction 3), and it would have to pay interest on however much is ultimately auctioned (transaction 4). As the loan from the BSP matures, the BSP will reduce outstanding TDF liabilities so sufficient RBs are circulating (or otherwise increase RBs as needed, such as by lending in repurchase agreement markets) in transaction 5. Then, in transaction 6, the BTr issues its own securities to fund the repayment. In transaction 7, the BTr repays the loan.

Note that for the BTr, the BSP, and private financial markets, the primary change is that interest on BTr liabilities has been explicitly set by the BSP. Because the TDF liabilities auctioned by the BSP in

---

[26] As the BSP's own literature on its operations states, "The Term Deposit Facility is a key liquidity absorption facility, commonly used by CBs for liquidity management. The TDF is used to withdraw a large part of the structural liquidity from the financial system to bring market rates closer to the BSP policy rate." (Bangko Sentral ng Pilipinas 2016, 5).

Table 23. Operations Involved in the ₱300 Billion Loan to the Government by the Bangko Sentral ng Pilipinas

Transaction	Effect on Interest Rate Corridor System (left side of Figures 7 and 8)	Effect on Bangko Sentral ng Pilipinas' Balance Sheet	
		A	L/E
(1) BSP credits BTr's account		Loan to BTr (+300)	BTr Acct (+300)
(2) BTr incurs a deficit	Shift SRB to the right		RBs (+300) BTr Acct (−300)
(3) BSP's TDF auctions drain excess RBs	Shift SRB to the left		RBs (−300) TDF (+300)
(4) BSP pays interest on new TDF balances			TDF (+int) Equity (−int)
(5) BSP reduces TDFs auctioned	Shift SRB to the right		RBs (+300) TDF (−300)
(6) BTr auction settles	Shift SRB to the left		RBs (−300) BTr Acct (+300)
(7) BTr repays loan principal to BSP		Loan to BTr (−300)	BTr Acct (−300)
(8) BSP remittances to BTr are lower by the interest paid on TDFs[a]			BTr Acct (−300−int) Equity int (+300+int)

A = assets, BSP = Bangko Sentral ng Pilipinas, BTr = Bureau of the Treasury of the government's Department of Finance, BTr Acct = BTr's account at BSP, int = size of the interest payment, L/E = liabilities and equity, RB = reserve balance, SRB = supply of RBs, TDF = Term Deposit Facility.

[a] The BSP does not actually debit the BTr's account in transaction (8), but rather the remittance transfer is less than it would have been in the absence of transaction (1).

Source: Authors.

transaction (3) are interest-bearing, the BSP reduces its remittances in kind in transaction (8).[27] For the BTr, it is as if it issued its own liabilities to financial markets at the rate set by the BSP. From the financial system's perspective, the result is to effectively swap BTr liabilities normally linked to the anticipated path of the BSP's target rate for TDFs at the BSP that earn roughly the BSP's target rate. Overall, the BSP's explicit backstop of the government securities market and its loan to the BTr show its own interest in ensuring the link remains between the BSP's target rate and interest rates on government liabilities.

As for its 26 March 2020 advance dividend payment to the government, BSP explains:

To further support the government in its fight against Coronavirus disease 2019 (COVID-19), the Bangko Sentral ng Pilipinas (BSP) will remit [PHP]20 billion as advance dividend to the National Government (NG). The advance dividends constitute 87% of the estimated total dividends based on the BSP's unaudited financial statements for the year 2020.

BSP will remit the [PHP]20 billion advance dividends today, 26 March 2020, through direct credit to the Treasurer of the Philippines-Treasurer Single Account, which is maintained with the BSP (Bangko Sentral ng Pilipinas 2020).

27 The BSP's loan to BTr is a zero-interest loan (Leyco 2020).

The BSP's advance dividend payment to the BTr is effectively directly financing the government, and repayment occurs as a reduction in kind of future remittances. The transactions involved in this ₱20 billion advance payment to the government are in Table 24, where transactions (2) through (4) are identical to those in Table 23. As with the 23 March 2020 repurchase agreement, once the national government incurs a deficit, the BSP will drain RBs to achieve its interest rate target within the corridor by auctioning interest-bearing TDF liabilities. When the BSP pays interest on TDF liabilities, this reduces its profits. Later on, the BSP will reduce its remittances by the combined amount of the advance and the interest paid on the new TDF liabilities. The advance dividend payment ultimately functions as if the BTr issued its own debt to the private sector at the TDF auction rate.

Table 24. Operations Involved in the ₱20 Billion Advance Dividend Payment to the Government by the Bangko Sentral ng Pilipinas

Transaction	Effect on Interest Rate Corridor System (left side of Figures 7 and 8)	Effect on Bangko Sentral ng Pilipinas' Balance Sheet	
		A	L/E
(1) BSP makes advance remittance to BTr			BTr Acct (+20) Equity (–20)
(2) BTr incurs a deficit	Shift SRB right		RBs (+20) BTr Acct (–20)
(3) BSP's TDF auctions drain excess RBs	Shift SRB left		RBs (–20) TDF (+20)
(4) BSP pays interest on new TDF balances			TDF (+int) Equity (–int)
(5) Later, BSP reduces remittances to BTr by amount of advance dividends and interest on new TDF balances[a]			BTr Acct (–20–int) Equity (+20+int)

A = assets, BSP = Bangko Sentral ng Pilipinas, BTr = Bureau of the Treasury of the government's Department of Finance, BTr Acct = BTr's account at BSP, int = size of the interest payment, L/E = liabilities and equity, RB = reserve balance, SRB = supply of RBs, TDF = Term Deposit Facility.

[a] The BSP does not actually debit the BTr's account in action (5), but rather the remittance transfer is less than it would have been in the absence of action (1) earlier.

Source: Authors.

As in the previous section's discussion of core points, the BTr cannot avoid paying interest on new debt created by deficits even when the BSP finances them directly. Because the BSP must issue its own interest-bearing liabilities in the meantime, it reduces remittances in kind and the BTr effectively pays roughly the BSP's interest rate target on new increases in the national debt. Overall, the reality of central bank's financing of government is not like printing money as discussed in textbooks and the financial press or even by most economists. Instead, the result is an increase in interest-bearing liabilities of the central bank, which the government ultimately services, much like if the government had issued the debt in the first place. The BSP's actions in the first months of the COVID-19 crisis illustrate the point that the primary rationale of central bank support of government is to keep interest rates on new debt lower or intervene to reduce liquidity problems, not to add more impact to the existing deficit.

C.   The Monetary Authority of Singapore and the Government's Drawdown of Reserves

The case of the Monetary Authority of Singapore (MAS) is equally interesting, but in an entirely different way. MAS is well known for its exchange rate-driven monetary policy strategy that sets an intermediate target of the Singapore dollar (S$) against a weighted basket of currencies to achieve a policy target for the inflation rate. At the tactical level, MAS notes that its Monetary and Domestic Markets Management Department, responsible for implementing monetary policy, is tasked with achieving the nominal effective exchange rate (NEER) target band via foreign exchange markets intervention as well as managing banks' abilities to settle payments and meet regulatory reserve requirements (Monetary Authority of Singapore 2013, 2). Of particular interest here is the Government of Singapore's "draw on the nation's reserves" to pay for COVID-19 support and how this is, in fact, an example of monetization of government deficits. This requires an explanation of some of the details in MAS's typical operations.

Throughout its own publications and speeches, MAS describes itself as an exchange rate targeting central bank, not an interest rate targeting central bank: "MAS' liquidity management framework therefore does not target any level of interest rate or money supply" (Monetary Authority of Singapore 2013, 8). Accordingly, it argues, "as MAS does not have an interest rate target, the borrowing and lending rates for the Standing Facility are market-determined" (p. 18). The ceiling for MAS's interest rate corridor (the Standing Facility Borrowing Rate [SFBR]) and the rate it pays on banks' RBs as the corridor's floor (the Standing Facility Deposit Rate [SFDR]) are set daily at +0.5% and –0.5% (though to this point not falling below 0%), respectively, from the day's market rate, rather than being policy variables for MAS.

This is true at a strategic level, but not at the tactical level of policy making. MAS obviously understands this and is usually clear in its own publications in this regard, but those without expertise in central bank operations may miss the subtleties. Consider the following passages in which MAS distinguishes intermediate targets from direct or operational targets:

> Unlike most central banks which target interest rates, MAS uses the nominal exchange rate as the intermediate target of monetary policy (Monetary Authority of Singapore 2018, 7; emphasis in original).

> Money Market Operations (MMOs) are conducted Daily by the Monetary and Domestic Markets Management Department (MDD) in MAS to manage liquidity within the banking system . . . . These are distinct from the implementation of exchange rate policy as MAS does not use domestic interest rates as a tool to carry out its exchange rate-centered monetary policy (Monetary Authority of Singapore 2018, 11).

In other words, there is a distinction to be made between decisions regarding where to set the NEER target range as set by monetary policy strategy—analogous to how a Taylor-type rule framework works in an interest rate target strategy at other central banks—and operations that achieve "an appropriate amount of liquidity in the banking system—sufficient to meet banks' demand for precautionary and settlement balances, but not excessive" (Monetary Authority of Singapore 2013, 8).

Recalling the first core point earlier in this chapter, at the tactical level of policy, central banks necessarily employ interest rate targets or target ranges, even if the placement of the target or target range is endogenous to, in MAS's case, an NEER target at the strategic level of policy. RBs in circulation exist only on the central bank's balance sheet; the quantity of RBs, and thus the interest rate paid to borrow them or earned when lending them, is not and cannot be something the market determines without a conscious choice by the central bank to accommodate. As Federal Reserve Bank of New York researchers put it, "the costs of reserves, both intraday and overnight, are policy variables. Consequently, a market for reserves does not play the traditional role of information aggregation and price discovery" (Martin and McAndrews 2008, 1). As with other central banks that are the monopoly supplier of RBs with no operational limit to its ability to do so, how much or how little precision MAS chooses to employ in accommodating banks' demand for RBs necessarily determines the market's rate.

Singapore private banks' demand for RBs arises from their need to meet required RB holdings against certain liabilities and to also have enough RBs to settle payments for customers and for their own payment obligations. This is standard for monetary policy implementation in other countries as well (though many do not require banks to hold a minimum quantity of RBs greater than 0). Banks' required RBs in Singapore are 3% of qualifying liabilities held on average during a 2-week computation period. After a 2-week lag, banks meet the requirement on average throughout a 2-week maintenance period (MAS's RB requirement is thus based on lagged reserve accounting). End-of-day RBs for a bank can fluctuate between 2% and 4% of the qualifying liabilities, as long as average RBs held across the period is at least 3%. Banks can also run intraday RBs down to 0 temporarily to settle payment obligations (Monetary Authority of Singapore 2013, 2014). In general, a minimum RB requirement met on average during a maintenance period generates a flatter region in DRB around the central bank's interest rate target for much of the period, but this flatter region largely evaporates by the period's end, leaving DRB much more inelastic.

Central banks must accommodate banks in the payments system, and they also must accommodate with some degree of flexibility banks' attempts to meet RB requirements (where applicable, since not all central banks impose RB requirements), all in order to avoid large swings in the market interest rate. In MAS's case,

> MAS carries out money market operations every morning at about 9:45am. The purpose of these operations is to ensure that there is an appropriate amount of liquidity in the banking system: sufficient to meet banks' demand for precautionary and settlement balances, but not excessive (Monetary Authority of Singapore 2013, 12).

> After deciding on the amount of liquidity to inject or withdraw from the system, as well as the instruments and tenors to transact in, MAS conducts an auction and transacts with Primary Dealers based on the distribution of liquidity in the banking system and the competitiveness of their bids (Monetary Authority of Singapore 2013, 13).

To reiterate, provision of "an appropriate amount of liquidity" is not possible without doing so consistent with an interest rate or an interest rate range. This is simply supply and demand. Everything that affects SRB is on MAS's balance sheet and thus can be accommodated or countered if MAS so chooses. Likewise, its choice to shift or not shift SRB are never in isolation from DRB. If it shifts SRB, then the market rate changes. If DRB shifts and MAS leaves SRB where it is, then MAS enabled the market rate to change. If the market rate does not change, then MAS enabled that as well by its decision to act or to not act upon whatever DRB did (if anything) relative to nonoperations-based changes to MAS's balance sheet (if any). The fact that DRB becomes very inelastic beyond what is necessary to settle payments and meet RB requirements further reinforces this (and is itself a product of MAS's liquidity requirements). The interest rate or interest rate range that MAS targets is endogenous to the needs of its NEER targeting strategy, but setting a target rate or a target rate range at the tactical level of policy is inherently impossible for it to avoid.[28] Of course, in MAS's case, because the corridor itself is set by the day's market rate that results from MAS's tactical operations—which it refers to as the reference rate—this corridor system enables greater swings in the "market" rate across days, but this is by MAS's own choices in designing its corridor system, liquidity regulations, and tactics, not something deriving from market forces.[29]

MAS has several tools beyond the standard repo operations with dealers and its standing facilities (SFBR and SFDR) for managing the quantity of RBs within its tactical target range for the reference rate. These are, namely,

(i)   inexpensive intraday credit (currently 0%);

(ii)   a term (28- and 84-day) repurchase facility for banks and finance companies;

(iii)   term (7-, 28-, and 84-day) lending and borrowing in US dollars against various possible types of collateral, which, if denominated in S$, can include "cash" (that is, a currency swap that drains RBs);

(iv)   a term renminbi facility for loans against S$ (a currency swap that drains RBs);

(v)   an overnight renminbi facility against S$ collateral which can also include "cash" (a currency swap that drains RBs); and

(vi)   MAS's own bills (MAS Bills) that have 4- or 12-week maturities, and also its own 6-month floating rate notes.

As MAS confirms, "the liquidity facilities allow MAS to fine-tune the liquidity in the system as necessary" (Monetary Authority of Singapore 2013, 17). Consequently, shifts in DRB from banks, or shifts in SRB from foreign exchange operations, changes in the private sector's desired holdings of currency, flows to and from the government's account, and/or anything else on MAS's balance sheet are accommodated or countered (that is, sterilized) as MAS chooses, and the resulting market interest rate and possible ranges in its volatility are inherently a result of those choices and the design of its corridor system, notwithstanding the fact that those choices are subservient to its NEER targeting strategy.

---

[28]   This is essentially the "compensation thesis" in Lavoie and Wang (2012).

[29]   MAS defines the reference rate—for which it sets its standing facilities' 0.5% above and below—as "the weighted average of successful bids for MAS's S$500 million overnight clean borrowing conducted during Money Market Operations on the same day, rounded to two decimal places." (See MAS: https://www.mas.gov.sg/monetary-policy/liquidity-facilities/mas-standing-facility [accessed 30 September 2020].) As the block quotes in the text from MAS (2013, 12–13) explain, MAS's operations are in the mornings, which thereby establish the standing facility rates for the day. So, standing facility rates (SFBR and SFDR) can rise or fall from day to day, but MAS's morning operations set them for any given day.

Figure 9 shows the overnight reference rate and MAS Standing Facilities data for 2019 and 2020 (through 30 September 2020). Values for the daily reference rate (Monetary Authority of Singapore 2013, 2014; calculated here as 0.5% below the reported SFBR) are shown for each day (thinner, light blue line) and as a 4-week moving average (thicker, dark blue line). The reported SFBR and SFDR are the dotted lines, here in the form of 4-week moving averages. From the graph, a fairly clear corridor for SFBR and SFDR appears between around 2.25% and 1.25% from January to September 2019, and between 1.75% and 0.75% from October 2019 to around February 2020. These are the values for the gold and red horizontal lines in the graph through February 2020 and could be near what MAS targeted for SFBR and SFDR through February 2020 to be consistent with its NEER target. Thereafter, as COVID-19 events took hold, MAS fairly abruptly allowed both rates to fall, with SFDR at its zero lower bound and SBDR usually between 0.5% and 0.75%. From January to September 2019, there is an apparent average target range between 1.5% and 2% as shown by the 4-week average reference rate. This appears to decline to 1.25%–2% from October 2019 to February 2020, and then slowly declines to 0%–0.25% by May 2020.

From Figure 9 and the above discussion of MAS's operations and liquidity requirements emerges a representation of MAS's corridor system, which is shown in Figure 10. The corridor set by SFBR and SFDR shifts up or down daily with changes in the standing facilities' reference rate (imarket in Figure 10). In Figure 9, MAS appears more interested in an average value over time for imarket, and appears to

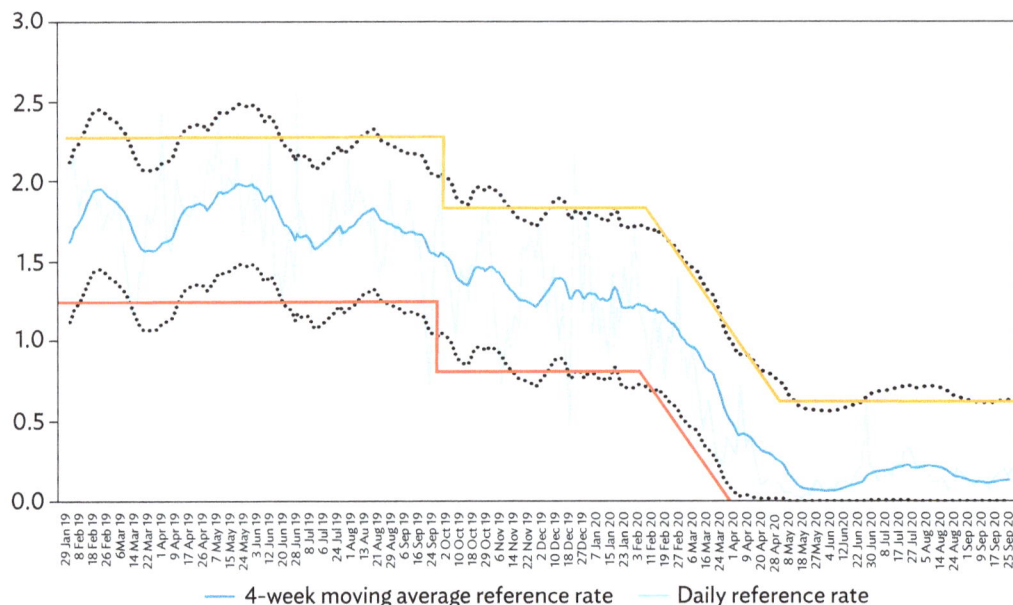

Figure 9. Monetary Authority of Singapore's Standing Facility Borrowing Rate, Standing Facility Deposit Rate, and Imputed Standing Facility Reference Rate, January 2019–September 2020

Notes: Upper and lower dotted lines are 4-week moving averages for the Standing Facility Borrowing Rate (SFBR) and Standing Facility Deposit Rate (SFDR), respectively. Gold and red lines are hypothesized average targeted values for SFBR and SFDR, respectively.

Sources: Monetary Authority of Singapore and authors' calculations.

target average imarket within a range that is not as wide as the corridor. DRB flattens somewhat within the range that banks hold RBs during most of the maintenance period in the left graph, providing MAS with a range of quantities of RBs that are consistent with an average target range. As the maintenance period comes to an end, nearly all of this flattened portion of DRB evaporates in the right graph, leaving MAS facing a more inelastic DRB.

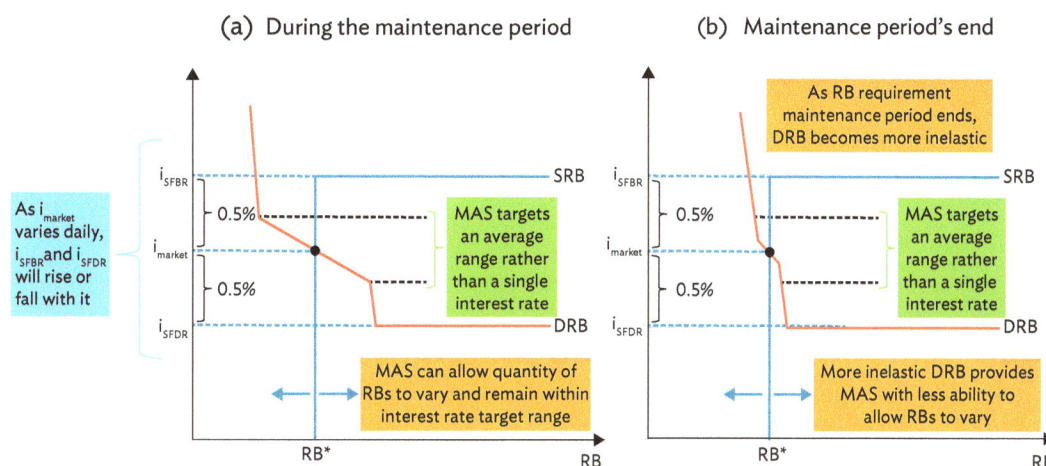

Figure 10. Monetary Authority of Singapore's Corridor System during the Maintenance Period and at the Maintenance Period's End

DRB = demand for RBs, i_{market} = reference rate, i_{SFBR} = Standing Facility Borrowing Rate, i_{SFDR} = Standing Facility Deposit Rate, MAS = Monetary Authority of Singapore, RB = reserve balance, SRB = supply of RBs.
Source: Authors.

The exceptions in which the overnight rate has increased or decreased significantly prove the rule. As MAS explains,

> In mid-September 1985 when there was a speculative attack on the Singapore dollar, MAS intervened in the foreign exchange market to buy the Singapore dollar against the US dollar but did not offset the liquidity drain of the intervention through money market operations. The intervention operation was left unsterilized, so as to reduce banking system liquidity and make it costly for speculators to cover their short Singapore dollar positions. . . . Overnight interest rates surged close to 100% per annum that day and hovered between 20–30% per annum for the following few days (Monetary Authority of Singapore 2013, 13).

> On the morning of 12 September 2001, following the terrorist attacks on New York City the night before, MAS injected [SG$]2.5 billion into the banking system to bring banks' cash balances with MAS to 4.5%, above the statutory minimum of 3%, to calm market participants and ensure the smooth functioning of all Singapore dollar markets. It was only after some calm had been restored to the market that MAS withdrew some of the liquidity late in the afternoon (Monetary Authority of Singapore 2013, 13).

Clearly MAS recognizes that its own actions created these significant swings in the overnight interest rate, not the market at the tactical level.

What do MAS's operations to set an interest rate target range at the tactical level consistent with its NEER targeting strategy have to do with monetization given that the Government of Singapore legally prohibits itself from incurring deficits? While it may not run deficits as typically understood, Singapore nonetheless issues government debt, and the details of how and why are very unique. As Singapore's Ministry of Finance explains,

> The Government of Singapore currently issues the following domestic securities for reasons unrelated to the government's fiscal needs:
>
> (i)   Singapore Government Securities (SGS) are issued to develop the domestic debt market;
>
> (ii)   Special Singapore Government Securities (SSGS) are nontradable bonds issued primarily to meet the investment needs of the Central Provident Fund (CPF), Singapore's national pension fund; and
>
> (iii)   Singapore Saving Bonds are introduced to provide individual investors with a long-term saving option that offers safe returns (Accountant-General's Department 2019, 3).

It confirms that, "under the Government Securities Act, the borrowing proceeds from the issuance of these securities cannot be spent and are invested" (p. 3). When the Government of Singapore raises funds from the issuance of Singapore Government Securities or Singapore Savings Bonds, or net inflows to CPF, these are all credits to its account(s) at MAS and an in-kind reduction in RBs held by Singapore's banks, consistent with the second core point discussed earlier in the chapter. Next, the funds are pooled together and "MAS converts these funds into foreign assets through the foreign exchange market" (Singapore Ministry of Finance n.d.). Note that this adds back the RBs, leaving no net change to RBs from bond issuance. The Government of Singapore Investment Corporation (GIC)[30] manages much of the government's international investments (the other "fund manager" being MAS, which manages the official foreign reserves) in a globally diversified portfolio, then takes over management of the foreign assets.[31]

While the government cannot spend proceeds of bond sales, it does have legal access to total net investment returns beyond the costs of servicing the securities and managing the investment portfolio. This Net Investment Returns Contribution (NIRC) is then additional annual funding for the government's budget. NIRC is composed of (i) up to 50% of annual Net Investment Income (NII) from interest and dividends (again, net of debt service and other expenses); and (ii) up to

---

[30]   GIC is "a private company wholly owned by the Government of Singapore. We do not own the assets we manage...." Further, "although we are government-owned and manage Singapore's reserves, our relationship with the government is that of a fund manager to a client." (GIC. https://www.gic.com.sg/faq/ [accessed 30 September 2020].)

[31]   As in the Accountant-General's Department description, CPF receives nonmarketable SSGS in exchange for the funds GIC invests. Essentially, CPF's holdings of SSGS provide it with legal authority to pay future benefit payments equal to revenues, interest from SSGS, and the value of the SSGS holdings. The SSGS holdings do not provide financial ability to pay, however, since CPF's SSGS holdings and interest payments from them exist only as internal accounting among different departments within the same government.

50% of annual Net Investment Returns (NIR), calculated as the real expected long-term capital gains (that is, after netting out anticipated long-term inflation) from the net of invested assets less liabilities (Singapore Ministry of Finance n.d.).[32] The NIRC values for 2018 and 2019 were S$16 billion (Accountant-General's Department 2019, 7) and S$17.2 billion (Singapore Ministry of Finance n.d.), or 3.25% of 2018 GDP and 3.4% of 2019 GDP, respectively.

Returning to MAS's operations, when the government spends its annual NIRC, this is a net increase in RBs. The NII portion is a credit to the government's account at MAS, while the offsetting operation is MAS acquiring foreign assets from GIC or adding to its own foreign investment portfolio (i.e., dividends and interest cash flows from GIC's and MAS's international investments are in foreign currencies).[33] The quantity of combined actual assets owned by MAS and/or the government (itself the owner of GIC) in fact remains unchanged; at most, there are asset transfers between the government via its own investments and MAS so that the full value of the NIRC is on MAS's balance sheet (if it was not already), while total holdings across the two remain the same.

Table 25 presents the case of NII where MAS's investments are the source of the interest cash inflows. Transaction (1) shows the interest income from MAS's global portfolio ("Inv Port" in the table) increasing MAS's equity. In transaction (2), MAS makes NII transfers to the government's account, reducing MAS's equity and raising the government's net worth. The government's spending is in transaction (3), here assumed to be payments to households, which raises household net worth and reduces the government's by the same amount. Because transaction (3) increased RBs, MAS sterilizes it in transaction (4) by issuing MAS Bills to banks. Following transaction (4), MAS will, of course, pay interest on its bills, ultimately reducing its remittances. (The operations are not dissimilar for NII paid from GIC's interest and dividend income, since these also come from international investments and, because it is wholly owned by the government, GIC's income is the government's income.) As noted above, and of particular interest, is that the government's spending of the NII proceeds does not reduce the balances in MAS's global portfolio. Instead, MAS's interest obligations on its MAS Bills become a cost relative to the returns that can be earned on this increased size of the investment portfolio. Overall, spending NII proceeds is equivalent to the government running a deficit without a bond sale—monetization—and MAS issuing its own bills to raise funds for the global investment portfolio. The net effect is as if the Government of Singapore ran a deficit, with its indirect debt service for MAS's new liabilities reducing future interest and dividend income in kind from the national reserves net of the cost of servicing liabilities.

The NIR portion is an outright credit to the government's account at MAS beyond assets held by MAS and/or GIC, since NIR does not arise from any cash flows to the investment portfolios or from asset sales. The actual mechanics are unreported, but, at most, NIR is merely an intragovernmental advance from the reserve fund(s) to MAS and the government's account that is made whole upon the funds' realization of capital gains in the future. Effectively, this is the same as beginning with transaction (2) in Table 25 and skipping transaction (1). While there is no increase in the investment

---

[32] Essentially, NIR is the expected average annual real return from capital gains.

[33] For simplicity, the discussion abstracts from Temasek Holdings, a third manager of Singapore government's reserves (in addition to GIC and MAS) focusing on long-term equity investments within and outside of Singapore. The Government of Singapore is the sole equity holder of Temasek.

portfolio (since transaction [1] is skipped), like NII, NIR does not reduce combined assets of the funds. Further, as with NII yet again, following transaction (4), MAS pays debt service on its additional liabilities, and then reduces remittances. The overall effect is again as if the government simply runs a deficit that MAS sterilizes rather than the government issuing its own bonds, which increases the costs of the existing global investment portfolio relative to its total future returns (both interest and capital gains).[34] In short, the NIR contribution may provide the legal authority for the government to spend, but the operational reality is the spending is "funded" when MAS credits the government's account as the law requires it to do.

Table 25. Monetary Authority of Singapore Credits Net Investment Income to the Government

Transaction	Government of Singapore		MAS		Banks		Households	
	A	L/E	A	L/E	A	L/E	A	L/E
(1) MAS receives interest on global investments			Inv Port (+)	Equity (+)				
(2) MAS credits government with NII	MAS Acct (+)	Net Worth (+)		Govt Acct (+) Equity (−)				
(3) Government spends (or cuts taxes)	MAS Acct (−)	Net Worth (−)		RBs (+) Govt Acct (−)	RBs (+)	HH Dep (+)	Dep (+)	Net Worth (+)
(4) MAS issues MAS Bills to sterilize RBs				RBs (−) MAS Bills (+)	RBs (−) MAS Bills (+)			

A = assets, Dep = deposits, Govt Acct = the government's account at the central bank on the central bank's liabilities, HH = household, Inv Port = investment portfolio, L/E = liabilities and equity, MAS = Monetary Authority of Singapore, Net Worth = assets minus liabilities, NII = net investment income, RB = reserve balance.

Source: Authors.

---

[34] Of course, given the government's regular auctions of SGS, it could also be that an SGS auction removes the excess RBs and MAS's sterilization via MAS Bill issuance is unnecessary. Note that this is effectively the government running a deficit and afterward issuing SGS, illustrating that its own bonds are for the purpose of aiding MAS's interest rate maintenance, not funding a deficit.

In response to COVID-19, the Government of Singapore is effectively doubling the size of its budget, with more than half of the total—more than S$100 billion—going to its COVID-19 response. The NIRC for 2020 is S$18.6 billion. The government is also drawing down S$54.5 billion from its national reserves, the portfolios of investments that originated from past government securities issuance, past surpluses, past government asset sales, and so on.[35] As with NIRC, actual operations for a drawdown are unreported, so it is unclear if it involves an actual sale of S$54.5 billion in assets to acquire the funds. If not, then it is simply a credit to the government's account at MAS, similar to the NIR portion of NIRC in transactions (2), (3), and (4) in Table 25. And, again, like the NIRC, the government's subsequent spending increases RBs that MAS will sterilize via increases in its own interest-bearing liabilities, for which the interest payments also reduce remittances to the government. If the drawdown is from a sale of foreign currency-denominated assets held by GIC, for instance, this functions like the NII portion of NIRC, again raising RBs, requiring sterilization operations and increased debt service from MAS, and ultimately reduced remittances to the government. Note that the actual size of the national reserves is unchanged in either case, and the operations are effectively the same as with crediting the government with NIR: the national reserves are unchanged, but their relative costs increase (or their net returns fall), because of additional debt service by MAS (MAS Bill issuances) and/or the government (SGS auctions) as is necessary to sterilize excess RBs.

To conclude, while a drawdown of national reserves to the casual observer may appear to be simply a drawdown of savings like any firm or household would, for a government with a central bank, this is in fact simply a credit to the government's account at the central bank, with the subsequent spending raising RBs that must either be drained and replaced by an interest-earning liability of the central bank (in a corridor system) or earn interest at the central bank's target rate. Thus, the drawdown of reserve funds by the Government of Singapore creates additional, interest-bearing liabilities for MAS, who then reduces remittances such that the government effectively pays this interest as if it had incurred new debt equal to the amount of the drawdown. Thus, a "reserve drawdown" for a government transacting through its account at the central bank is operationally the same thing as a deficit that results in new debt outstanding along with new debt service requirements. While so-called prefunding likely appears to many to be "better housekeeping" (including perhaps to international governance institutions such as the International Monetary Fund), operationally there is no way around the accounting fact that either the Government of Singapore or MAS (or both) will end up with more interest-bearing liabilities outstanding. Finally, unlike when the private sector draws down its own savings or investments, for a country with a central bank that creates its own liabilities in its own currency without prior funding or concerns for its own solvency in its own currency, a reserve drawdown does not reduce the central bank's assets, which means it is not the assets that are necessary for the spending in the first place, but rather simply the legal authorization or requirement from the government that the central bank credit the government's account.

---

[35]   2020 NIRC and national reserves drawdown figures can be found in several sources, such as Kurohi (2020).

D.   The Monetization Debate in the People's Republic of China

A heated debate emerged in the PRC in May 2020 on whether or not the People's Bank of China (PBoC) should monetize the national government's deficits. Liu Shangxi, President of the Academy of Fiscal Science and member of the PRC's top political advisory body, argued that "monetization of the fiscal deficit will ease the government's tight financing conditions." He further suggested that the government could avoid the crowding out effect in financial markets even as the deficit reached a multiyear high as a percentage of GDP (Liu 2020). Numerous others countered this view. Ma Jun, a member of PBoC's monetary policy committee referred to "direct printing of money" as the source of asset price bubbles and hyperinflation (Ma 2020). Wu Xiaoling, former deputy governor of PBoC and current Vice Chair of the Financial and Economic Committee of the National People's Congress, argued that "currently, the Chinese [government bond] market has plenty of room for government bonds" (Wu 2020). The previous sections of this chapter can shed light on these differing points of view by walking through the three core points and applying, where possible, the experiences of the Philippines and Singapore.

PBoC's operations lie somewhere between the Philippines' BSP and Singapore's MAS. It runs an interest rate corridor system for which it announces both ceiling and floor rates similar to the BSP rather than allowing them to vary across days, but it also allows interest rates to vary within the corridor on average and uses numerous tools at different maturities to achieve a target range on average, similar to MAS (He and Jia 2020). Unlike the other two central banks, PBoC's interest rate targeting operations also occur within a significantly wider corridor (for instance, during January through May 2020 the width of the corridor was 2.6%), enabling PBoC's target rate range changes to occur without requiring PBoC to announce changes to the corridor itself. Further, PBoC makes more frequent use of changes in RB requirements than is typical for other central banks, and its operations are across a broader range of maturities that appear to tie interbank and repo rates out to 1 year (Felipe and Fullwiler 2020b).

As noted earlier, the Government of the PRC employs a TSAS that does not make use of correspondent bank accounts, unlike, say, the US before the Lehman Brothers bankruptcy (He and Jia 2020).[36] The TSAS leaves daily changes to the government's account at PBoC as a significant source of autonomous changes to PBoC's balance sheet, and leaves PBoC with the task of sterilizing these changes as necessary in order to achieve the policy target range. Figure 11 shows monthly averages for the PBoC's balance sheet (in billions of Chinese yuan) categorized by the change to currency and the government account together, which are the two primary autonomous portions of the PBoC's balance sheet (red columns), the change to RBs (blue columns), and the negative of the sum of changes to claims on financial institutions, other assets, and other liabilities (green columns).[37] The changes to RBs (monthly averages) are implicitly consistent with achieving the PBoC's interest rate target range.

---

[36]   See Kelton [Bell] (2000) and Tymoigne (2014) on the Treasury Tax and Loan account system in place until 2008 in the US.
[37]   PBoC publishes its balance sheet monthly.

Figure 11. Changes to the Balance Sheet of the People's Bank of China, February 2019–May 2020
(Monthly averages)

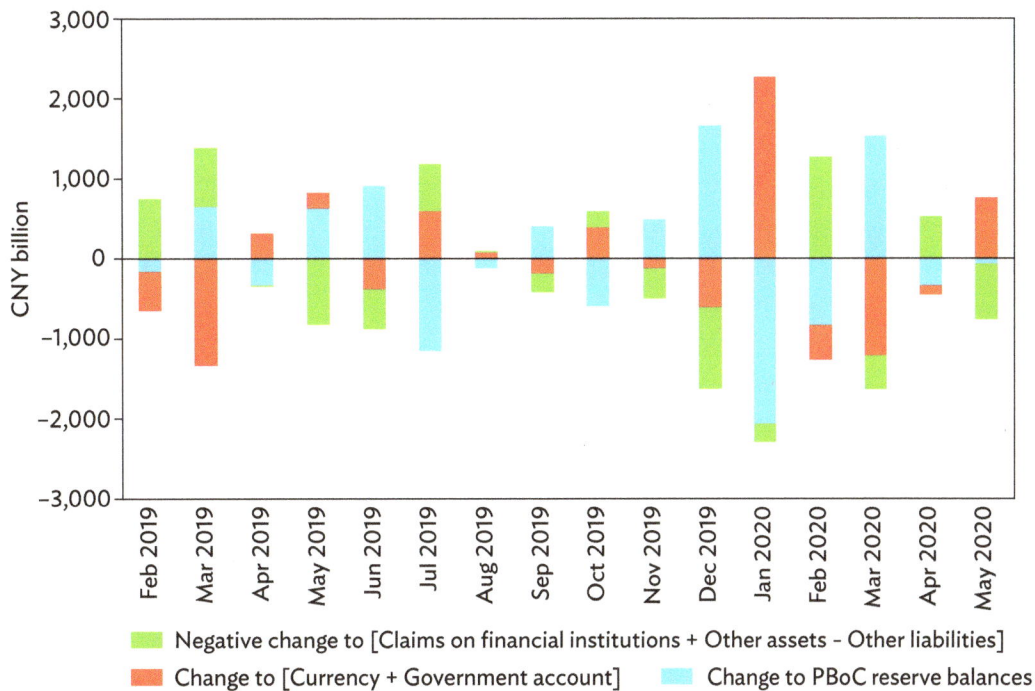

Negative change to [Claims on financial institutions + Other assets - Other liabilities]

Change to [Currency + Government account]   Change to PBoC reserve balances

CNY = yuan, PBoC = People's Bank of China.

Sources: People's Bank of China and authors' calculations.

The autonomous changes to currency and the government's account are changes to RBs (negative or positive) that would occur if PBoC did not sterilize them. The operations of PBoC (reported as claims on financial institutions, other assets, and other liabilities) adjust the quantity of RBs such that the quantities in the figure above and below 0 are roughly the same in absolute value and thus the netted value is close to 0.[38]

Consistent with the three core points discussed in the first part of this chapter, the PBoC sets an interest rate target within a corridor system and government spending, revenues, and bond sale settlement all occur via the government's account on the PBoC's balance sheet. As with the BSP and MAS, therefore, any monetization operations by the PBoC of government debt would necessarily require it to allow the overnight interest rate to fall to the rate it pays on RBs (for PBoC, this is the rate paid on excess RBs, since RBs required against liabilities do not earn interest), increase this rate, and/or issue its own interest-bearing liabilities. Yet again, monetization in the sense of creating noninterest bearing RBs is not operationally possible without a zero interest rate target policy. Government

---

[38] Claims on financial institutions are many times larger than both "other assets" and "other liabilities." Other items on the balance sheet, including claims on government, foreign exchange, foreign liabilities, and bonds issued varied little, at least at a monthly frequency during this period.

deficits are accompanied by interest-bearing liabilities in some combination from the central bank or government.

This is verified by the PBoC's Open Market Operations Office, which explained in its Announcement of Open Market Operations No. 124 [2020] on 29 June 2020 that, "Due to growing fiscal expenditure at the end of the month, the liquidity is adequate at a reasonable level in the current banking system. The People's Bank of China decides not to conduct reverse repo operations on June 29, 2020" (PBoC 2020). The PBoC calls its repurchase agreement lending operations "reverse repo operations," consistent with private sector practice, but opposite of the practice at the Federal Reserve and other central banks for which "repo" refers to adding RBs and "reverse repo" refers to draining them. Consequently, the 29 June 2020 statement simply and matter-of-factly informs that the government's deficit is providing the RBs to accommodate banks' DRB within the desired portion of the PBoC's target range within the interest rate corridor, such that the PBoC's own operations are unnecessary. The end-of-month deficits mentioned in the statement did not raise interest rates, but instead added RBs to keep the interbank rate from rising out of the PBoC's target range. Far from printing money, these deficits funded via additional RBs were simply integrated into the PBoC's normal interest rate management procedures. Overall, there may not be a more succinct public statement by any central bank in any historical period that more clearly illustrates the first two core points of this chapter as they occur in practice.

As for the third core principle, whether or not it is desirable for the PBoC to engage in monetization will depend on whether there is sufficient liquidity in the government bond markets to bring the yield curve on government bonds in line with the anticipated path of the central bank's interest rate target, and, if so, whether or not the central bank prefers bond markets to have an even lower anticipated path of its target rate. Wu Xiaoling's (2020) op-ed expressed essentially this view for the PBoC:

> If there is a problem with market liquidity, the central bank will buy and sell government bonds in the secondary market to provide liquidity.
>
> The biggest advantage of the People's Bank of China buying and selling government bonds from the secondary market is that it can form the yield curve of government bonds and provide a risk-pricing benchmark for the financial market.

She therefore concluded that the Chinese market for government bonds was sufficiently liquid, having "plenty of room" for more bond issuance, while confirming the PBoC's ability to manage the yield curve if it were to at some later date determine that the two reasons for a central bank to support government liabilities discussed in section VI.A applied.

Figure 12 shows monthly averages for the interbank overnight rate that the PBoC manages with rates on government securities across the yield curve for January through May 2020. The treasury rates decline from January through April with the interbank overnight rate, and then increase with the interbank rate's slight rise in May. The May increases in government treasury rates are larger than for the overnight rates, suggesting further anticipated rate increases from the PBoC. Consistent with Wu, the PRC's treasury rates did not move in a way inconsistent with the PBoC's average target rate for the interbank overnight rate.

The analysis here suggests flaws in the arguments both for and against monetization in the PRC's debate. Central bank purchases of government securities are not direct printing of money—they are an exchange of interest-earning government liabilities for interest-earning central bank liabilities. While the size of a deficit could surely be too large with respect to a given inflation target, whether the central banks or the government's interest-earning liability accompanies it is not a difference of macroeconomic significance, much less the knife-edge point between price stability and hyperinflation. Crowding out does not apply here—from the simple accounting in Table 22, a government deficit adds private saving rather than withdrawing it, while a bond market backstopped by the PBoC even indirectly means that interest rates on government debt are driven by monetary policy strategy, not savers and borrowers of loanable funds.

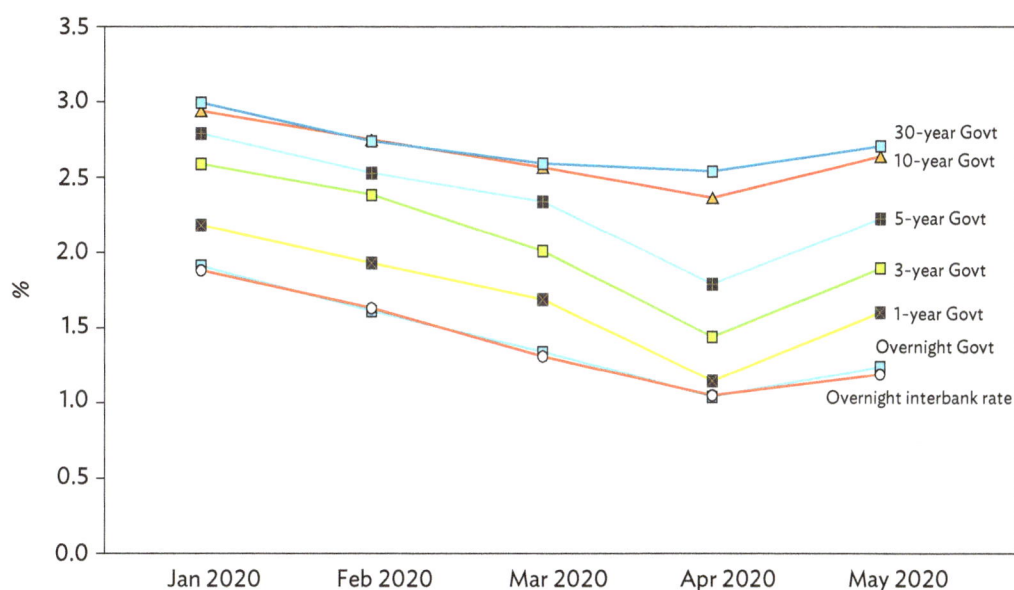

Figure 12. Interest Rates for Interbank Overnight Lending and Government Bonds, January 2020–May 2020

Govt = government.
Note: Data are monthly averages.
Source: People's Bank of China.

E.   Conclusions

The main argument of this chapter is that monetization does not occur in the way that most have learned about it, which includes economists and lay people alike. Direct printing of money as commonly understood is not operationally possible. In a corridor interest rate targeting system, the central bank's purchases of government debt are sterilized by an offsetting reduction in the central bank's assets or an increase in its own interest-bearing liabilities. In a floor system, the central bank can sterilize government debt through the interest it pays on RBs. Monetization simply cannot be the macroeconomic equivalent of adding "jet fuel" to government deficits. This means that monetization is not worth fearing, but it also means that it is not a solution in itself for an economy that is growing too slowly.

Monetization already happens quite regularly, often going unnoticed. Singapore's example illustrates this well. Beyond the examples in this chapter, the experiences of the ECB, the Federal Reserve, and Japan in the 2000s and 2010s demonstrate that printing money to create inflation is not as easy as economics textbooks claim. Tepid recoveries from COVID-19 in countries that appear in Table 21 should similarly reinforce this lesson. But old theories die hard even when they are inapplicable, and the fearmongers (again, economists and noneconomists alike) appear without exception even now whenever central bank monetization of government debt appears to have a likelihood greater than zero, or worse still if it is announced as official policy.

This chapter's caveat on monetization having no quantitative effect is that central banks can set the yield curve on domestic currency government debt. In countries with very liquid bond markets, they are already doing this and have been doing so for decades, indirectly monetizing government debt as a counterparty and/or backstop to primary dealers in order to enable competitive, liquid markets in which the cost of funds for the marginal trader is roughly the anticipated path of the central bank's target rate. While monetization does not have a quantitative effect beyond the deficit itself, an interest rate effect is obviously possible if the central bank chooses to bring down the interest rates on government debt below such levels or provides market liquidity when government debt markets are short of it.

The above notwithstanding, perceptions and understandings are evolving, if slowly. In September 2020, as the Philippines rewrote laws to allow the BSP to lend even greater amounts to the BTr, and as Indonesia had earlier written laws to both allow BI to directly purchase government debt in the primary market and then proposed another law (since abandoned) to also increase the influence of the Finance Ministry in monetary policy strategy, Standard & Poor's response was, "We have not seen signs that increased government bond purchases have damaged central bank credibility in India, Indonesia, and the Philippines. Inflation and interest rates have not picked up in these economies, and exchange rate changes have been modest so far" (quoted in Noble 2020). There are obvious continuing concerns for countries that are not able to withstand or otherwise avoid negative macroeconomic impacts of significant exchange rate depreciations, but it is well past time for recognizing that exchange rates are much more complex than nearly any theory suggests, much less simplistically presuming a direct causation from larger developing country government deficits and debt to exchange rate depreciation, fiscal crisis, and so on.

Chapter VII

An Analysis of Changes in Sectoral Balances and Private Sector Financial Positions in 2020

The ADB COVID-19 Policy Database compiled policy actions of governments and categorized these actions according to their differences in operational details and financial statement effects. Financial statement effects either create more debt or equity for the recipient, which also entails transfers of financial risks. In section VII.A, the study uses the sector financial balances (SFBs) approach to understand how the pandemic and government policies affected the sectors, particularly the domestic private sector. Section VII.B then decomposes the changes in the private sector into subsectors—households, nonfinancial firms, and the financial sector. A discussion follows in section VII.C of what it means if the private sector balance improves due to a government deficit. Lastly, in section VII.D, the study further analyzes the domestic private sector's financial position by looking at changes in leverage and financial survival constraint measures.

A. Introduction to Sector Financial Balances and Flow-of-Funds Accounts

From basic accounting principles, one person's spending is another person's income. Applying this in an economy, financial flows comprise a closed system. It is not possible, for instance, for every country to have a current account surplus; if one country has a current account surplus, then at least one other country has a current account deficit. Equivalently, if one sector of an economy has a surplus, at least one other sector must be in deficit.

Using annual and quarterly flow-of-funds reports from various economies, the study computes the SFBs for nonfinancial businesses (hereafter, firms), the financial sector, the household sector, the government, and the capital account balance (the net financial position of the rest of the world vis-à-vis the economy). The following simple identities define the SFBs and their flow-of-funds-based relationships to one another:

$$\text{Domestic private balance} \equiv \text{Household sector balance} + \text{Firm sector balance} + \text{Financial sector balance} \tag{1}$$

$$\text{Government balance} \equiv \text{Tax revenues} - \text{Government spending (including debt service)} \tag{2}$$

$$\text{Capital account balance} \equiv - \text{Current account balance} \qquad (3)$$
$$\text{Domestic private balance} + \text{Government sector balance} + \text{Capital account balance} \equiv 0 \qquad (4)$$

To illustrate, the analysis will use the Republic of Korea (ROK) as an example. Figure 13 shows SFBs using equation (4) for the ROK during 2009–2020. As equation (4) shows, the sum of the sector financial balances is 0 (financial flows are a closed system), thus the three SFBs generate mirror images above and below 0 in every quarter in the figure. It is clear that the SFBs drastically changed during the onset of the COVID-19 crisis from the first quarter (Q1) to Q2 2020. The previous quarters before the crisis were mostly characterized by government surpluses, domestic private sector surpluses, and capital account deficits (current account surpluses). In 2020, however, the government incurred large deficits averaging 6.9% of GDP, and the domestic private sector had surpluses averaging 8.3% of GDP. This historically large government deficit is a deviation from the ROK's typical pattern of consistent current account surpluses mirrored by domestic private sector surpluses, with the government's budget position mostly in surplus but also often a residual of the net of the other two sector balances.

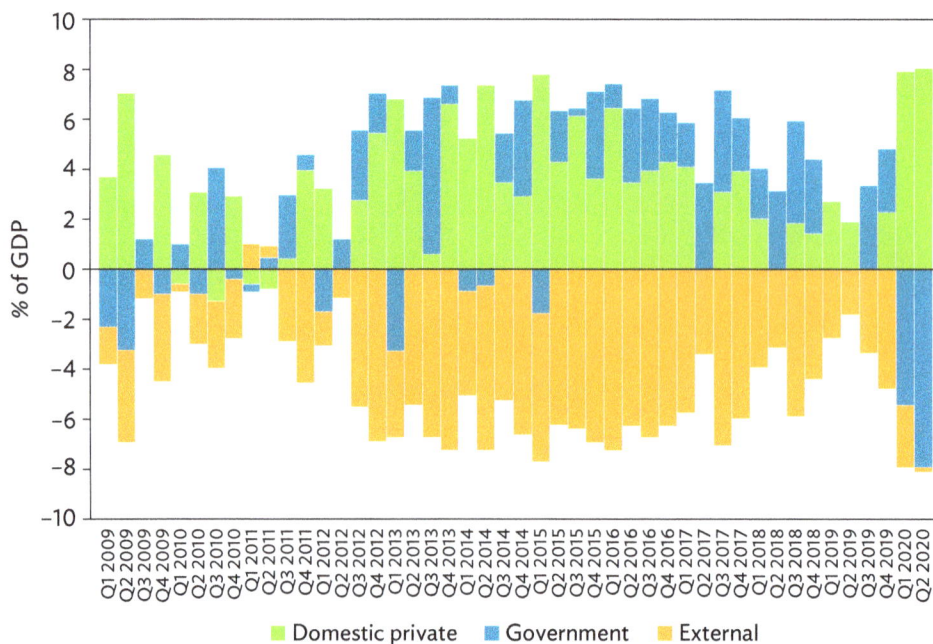

Figure 13. Sectoral Financial Balances, Republic of Korea, Q1 2009–Q2 2020

GDP = gross domestic product, Q = quarter.

Note: Sectoral financial balances were computed for each sector using flow-of-funds data.

Source: Authors' calculations based on the Republic of Korea's flow-of-funds data from CEIC (accessed 1 February 2021).

A useful way to visualize the inherent interactions of the SFBs is in Figure 14, which presents two axes and a bisecting line that together generate the sector financial balances map (SFBM).[39] The horizontal axis is the current account balance (CA) and the vertical axis is the government balance (GB). The diagonal dotted line bisects the graph through the origin—the domestic private sector balance (DPB) is 0 on every point along this line. For the SFBM, it is useful to substitute the negative of the current account balance from equation (3) into equation (4) and then rearrange as follows:

Domestic private balance ≡ Current account balance – Government sector balance   (5)

Using the abbreviations in the figure, equation (5) becomes

$$DPB \equiv CA - GB \qquad (6)$$

Figure 14 visually represents the logic of equations (5) and (6): the area to the northwest of the DPB = 0 line is where DPB < 0 since CA < GB, while the area to the southeast of DPB = 0 is where DPB > 0 since CA > GB.

Figure 14. Sector Financial Balances Map

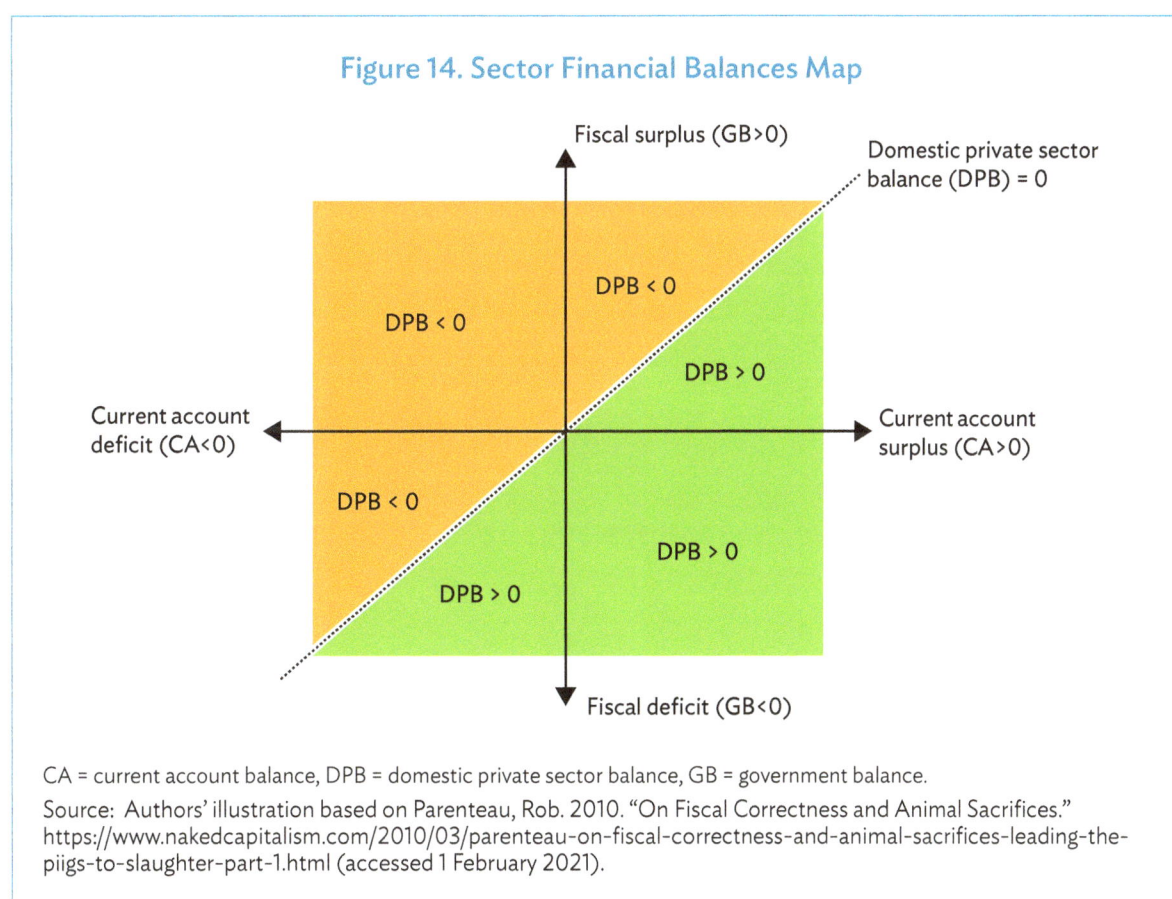

CA = current account balance, DPB = domestic private sector balance, GB = government balance.

Source: Authors' illustration based on Parenteau, Rob. 2010. "On Fiscal Correctness and Animal Sacrifices." https://www.nakedcapitalism.com/2010/03/parenteau-on-fiscal-correctness-and-animal-sacrifices-leading-the-piigs-to-slaughter-part-1.html (accessed 1 February 2021).

---

[39]   The SFBM originally appeared in Parenteau (2010).

Figure 15 plots the quarterly SFBs of the ROK for the period 2009–2020 in the SFBM. For most of 2009–2019, the ROK had a combination of government surplus, current account surplus, and domestic private sector surplus. However, in the first two quarters of 2020, the ROK incurred significantly high government deficits and had smaller current account surpluses.

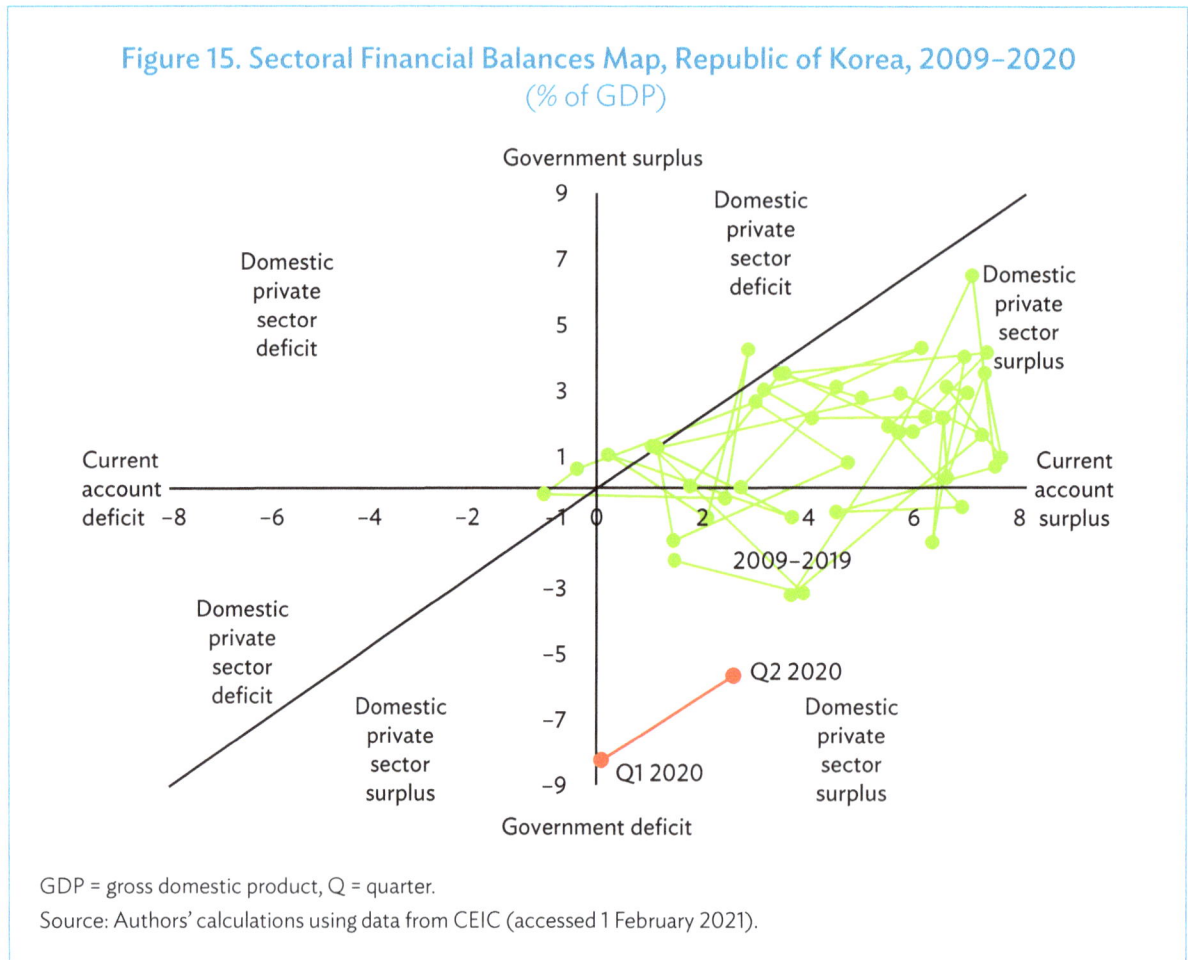

Figure 15. Sectoral Financial Balances Map, Republic of Korea, 2009–2020
(% of GDP)

GDP = gross domestic product, Q = quarter.
Source: Authors' calculations using data from CEIC (accessed 1 February 2021).

Figure 16 presents the SFBs of more economies for Q4 2019 and Q2 2020 using the SFBM. In Q4 2019, a majority of the economies had a domestic private sector surplus and a current account surplus. In Q2 2020, these economies moved southwest on the map, which corresponds to a higher government deficit, higher domestic private surplus, and small or negative current account surplus. As shown in Table 26, government deficit for these economies averaged 12.37% in Q2 2020 compared to 1.37% in Q4 2019. This was expected after economies released economic packages to support the private sector. The governments' deficits are the private sectors' surpluses. Figure 17 shows the SFBs of selected economies whose current account surpluses normally drive the domestic private sector. In 2020, these countries switched to the government sector driving the domestic private sector.

Figure 16. Sectoral Financial Balances Map, Selected Economies
(% of GDP)

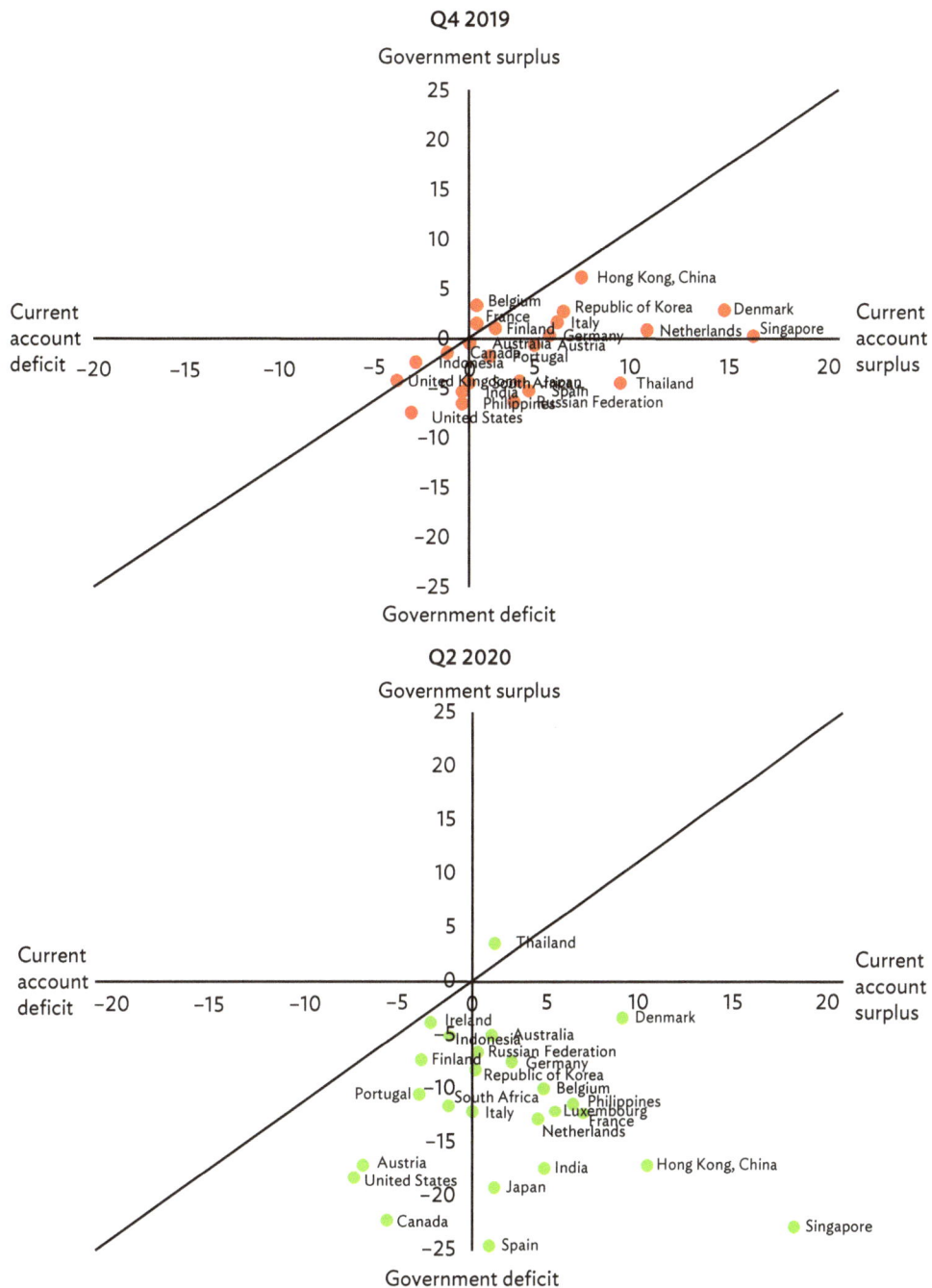

Q4 2019

Government surplus

Current account deficit

Current account surplus

Government deficit

(data points labeled: Hong Kong, China; Belgium; France; Finland; Republic of Korea; Italy; Denmark; Germany; Netherlands; Singapore; Australia; Austria; Canada; Portugal; Indonesia; United Kingdom; South Africa; India; Spain; Thailand; Philippines; Russian Federation; United States)

Q2 2020

Government surplus

Current account deficit

Current account surplus

Government deficit

(data points labeled: Thailand; Ireland; Indonesia; Australia; Russian Federation; Finland; Germany; Republic of Korea; Denmark; Belgium; Philippines; Portugal; South Africa; Luxembourg; France; Italy; Netherlands; Austria; United States; India; Hong Kong, China; Japan; Canada; Singapore; Spain)

GDP = gross domestic product, Q = quarter.

Source: Authors' calculations using flow-of-funds data from Eurostat at https://ec.europa.eu/eurostat/web/sector-accounts/data/database and CEIC, except for Hong Kong, China; India; Indonesia; the Philippines; the Russian Federation; Singapore; South Africa; and Thailand, which were estimated using national accounts data (accessed 1 February 2021).

Figure 17. Sector Financial Balances, Selected Economies, Q1 2018–Q2 2020
(% of GDP)

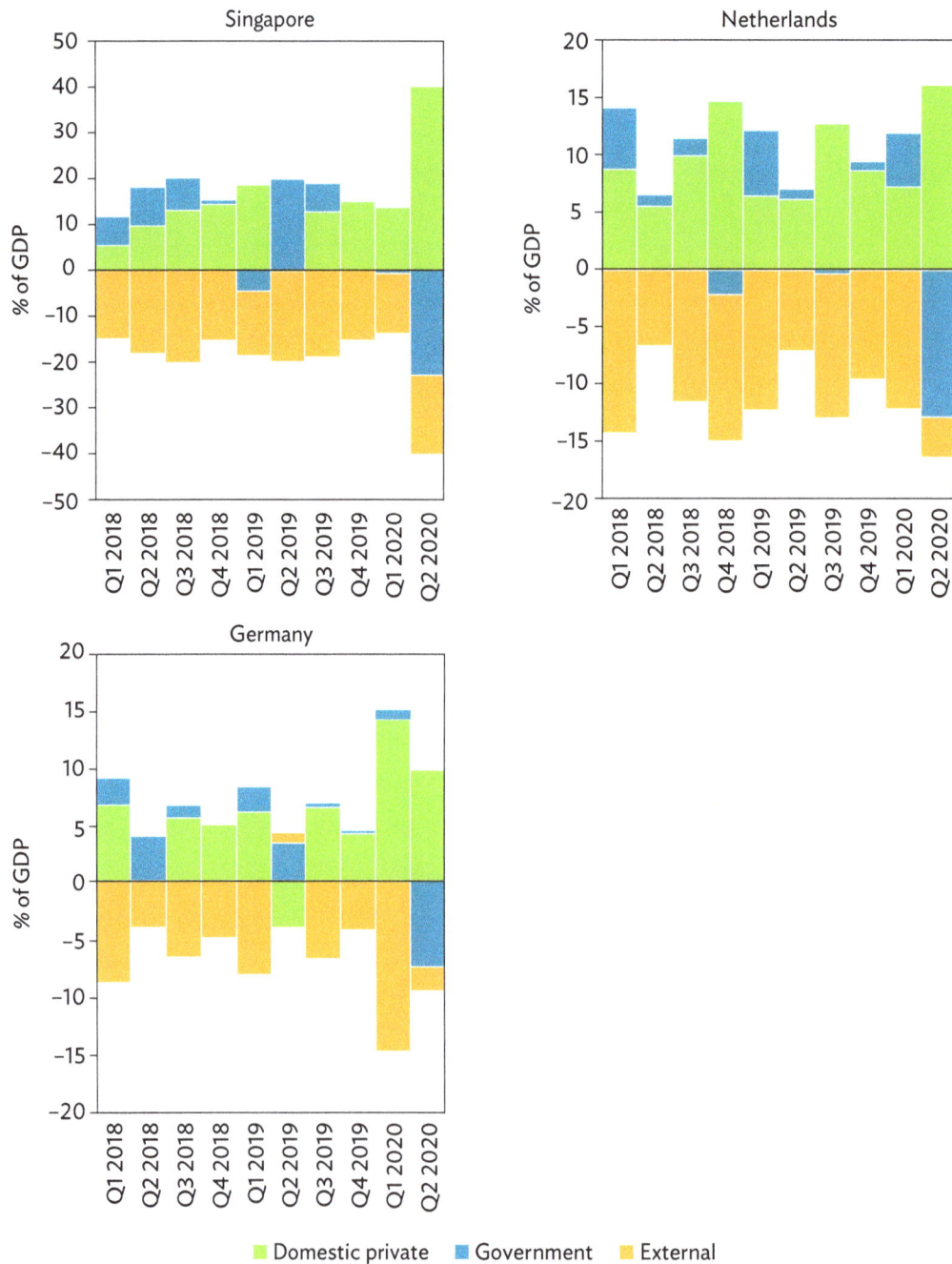

GDP = gross domestic product, Q = quarter.

Source: Authors' calculations using data from CEIC (accessed 1 February 2021).

Table 26. Average Sector Financial Balances
(% of GDP)

Quarter	DPB	Government	CA
Q4 2019	3.90	−1.37	2.52
Q2 2020	13.71	−12.37	1.35

CA = current account balance, DPB = domestic private sector balance, GDP = gross domestic product, Q = quarter.

Note: Data include economies listed in Figure 16.

Source: Authors' calculations using flow-of-funds data from Eurostat at https://ec.europa.eu/eurostat/web/sector-accounts/data/database and CEIC, except for Hong Kong, China; India; Indonesia; the Philippines; the Russian Federation; Singapore; South Africa; and Thailand, which were estimated using national accounts data (accessed 1 February 2021).

Box VII.1. Flow-of-Funds Accounts and National Income Accounts

Flow-of-funds accounts are produced by national statistics or central banks and supplement national accounts in measuring economic activity across economic sectors. These are the important differences between the flow-of-funds and national income accounts:[a]

(i)   National income accounts do not collect data on financial transactions, but flow-of-funds accounts do. Financial transactions include borrowing, lending, or changes in cash balances.

(ii) National income accounts present current flow of final expenditure, output, and income and do not show intermediate transactions. On the other hand, flow-of-funds accounts may capture intermediate intersectoral transactions and transactions involving assets generated in past periods.

(iii) In flow-of-funds accounts, all sectors can save and invest; however, in national income accounts, consumer durable expenditures are considered current expenditure and not an investment activity.

In computing sector financial balances, flow-of-funds and national accounts can both be used. The flow-of-funds approach provides a direct way of computing the sector balances since flow-of-funds accounts already provide measures on net acquisition of financial assets (i.e., changes in financial assets less changes in financial liabilities) for all sectors including the external sector (e.g., current account). The flow-of-funds approach further allows decomposition of the private sector balance into household, firms, and the financial sector balances. The national accounts approach of computing sector balances involves using figures for government deficit (GB) and current account balance (CA) and the identity $DPB \equiv CA - GB$ to derive domestic private sector balances (DPB).

---

[a]   Barbosa-Filho (2018) provides a detailed discussion using a social accounting matrix and integrates data from the National Income and Product Accounts published by the Bureau of Economic Analysis and the Flow-of-Funds Accounts or Financial Accounts of the United States (US) published by the US Federal Reserve.

Box VII.2. Countries' Signature Patterns of Sector Financial Balances

Countries tend to pursue different macroeconomic policy mixes that result in a typical signature pattern of sector financial balances, as seen in the charts below for India, Indonesia, and Germany. These patterns may be driven by fiscal rules, trade policies, or overall economic growth trends. The first chart for each country shows the financial balances for all three sectors—domestic private, government, and external—while the second chart shows only the two most dominant sectors interacting in the economy.

India has larger domestic private sector surpluses relative to its current account deficits, and its domestic private sector surpluses are matched by persistent government deficits. Unlike India, the pattern in Indonesia is one of persistent government account deficits matched by current account deficits, leaving domestic private sector balances near zero. Germany, on the other hand, has a similar pattern to the Republic of Korea (Figure 13), with persistent domestic private sector surpluses that are matched by large current account surpluses.

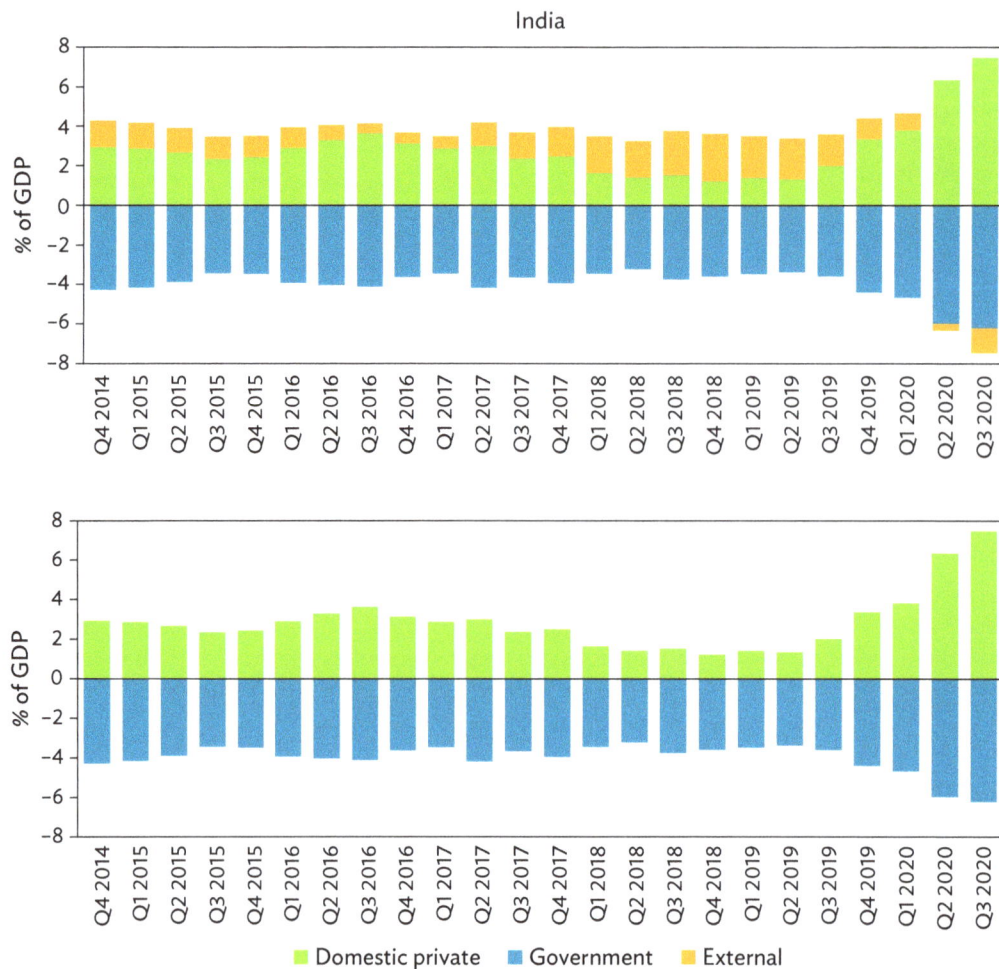

India

Domestic private   Government   External

continued on next page

Box VII.2 *continued*

Indonesia

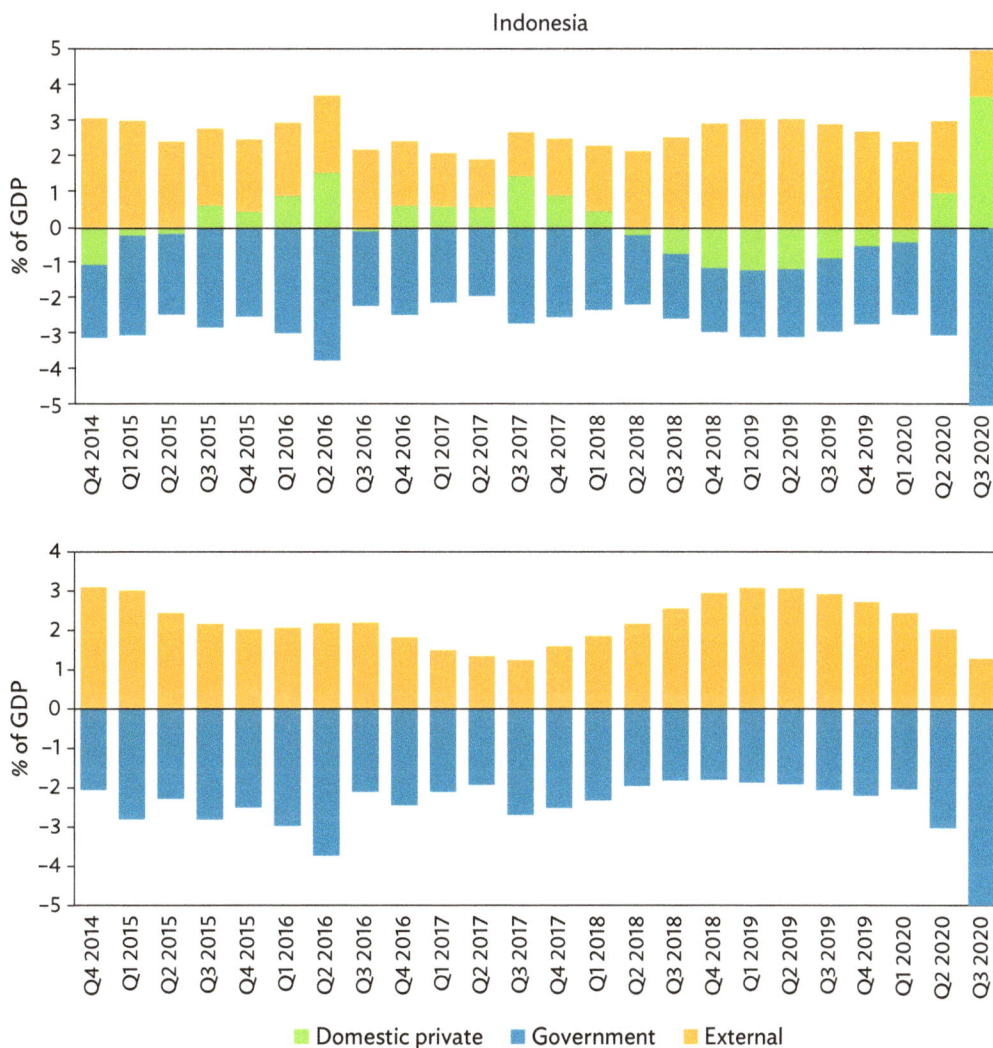

Domestic private ■ **Government** ■ **External**

continued on next page

Box VII.2 *continued*

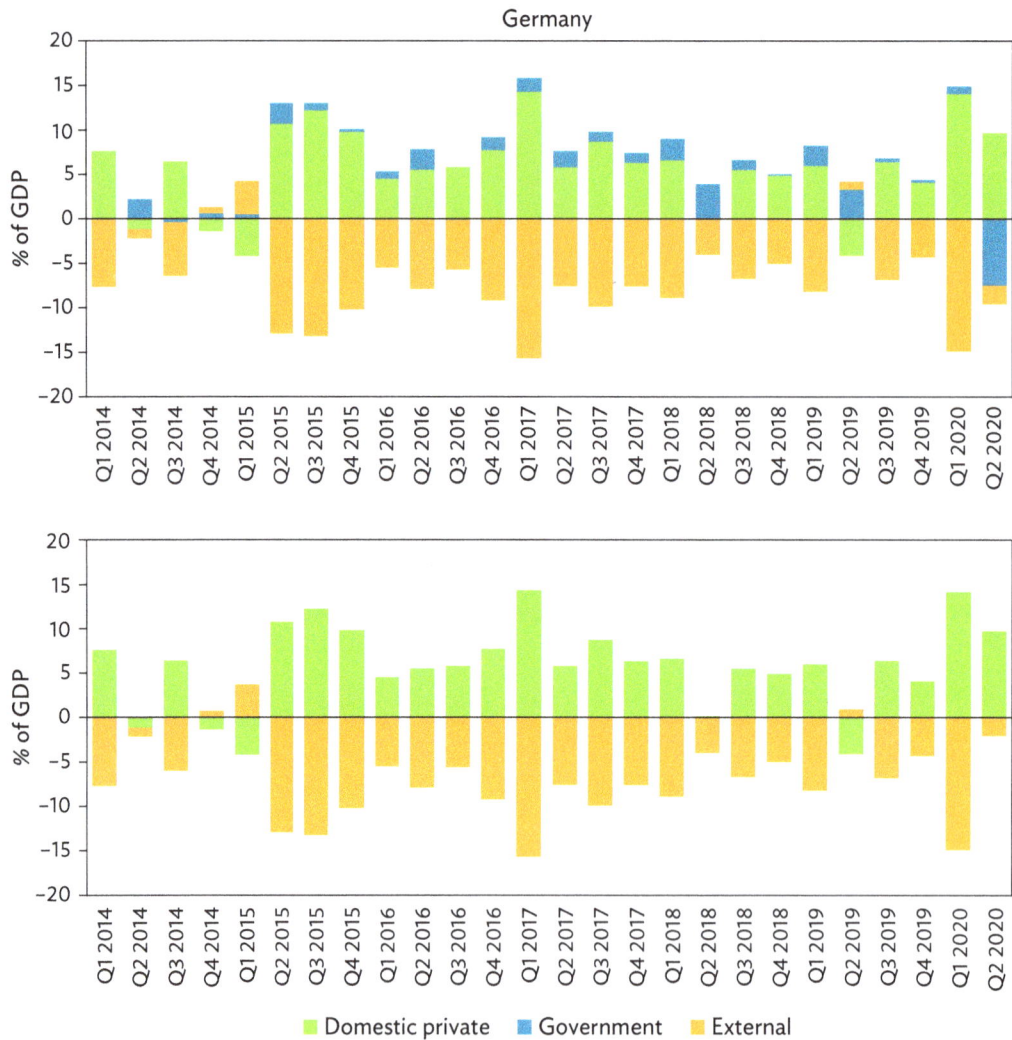

Germany

GDP = gross domestic product, Q = quarter.

Source: Authors' calculations using data from CEIC with seasonal adjustment for India and Indonesia and Eurostat for Germany at https://ec.europa.eu/eurostat/web/sector-accounts/data/database (accessed 1 February 2021).

B.   Decomposing the Domestic Private Sector Balance

Most countries in the early stages of the pandemic have seen significant increases in their domestic private sector balances. However, it is critical to understand which parts of the domestic private sector are experiencing these increases. The sector balances of the firms, households, and financial sector can be computed using flow-of-funds data. The sum of the sector balances of these three sectors is the total domestic private sector balance. It is important to note that transactions within these three subsectors do not affect the total domestic private sector balance.

Figure 18 shows the decomposition of the domestic private sector balances of Germany, the ROK, and the UK. The household sectors in these countries usually have positive balances, while the firm sector is either negative or alternates between positive and negative balances. In all three countries, the household sectors had significantly higher positive balances in 2020 compared to its usual balances in past years. In Q1 and Q2 2020, the ROK's household sector had an average surplus equivalent to 14.1% of GDP. This represents a significant increase from 2019 when the household sector surplus averaged 4.7% of GDP. The firm sector in the ROK had a higher deficit in the first half of 2020 averaging 6.2% of GDP compared to 3.1% in 2019. Meanwhile, no significant change is seen for the financial sector.

Decomposing domestic private sector balances using available flow-of-funds data reveals a consistent pattern for the economies shown in Table 27: all economies experienced a significant increase in household sector surplus in the first half of 2020. This can be explained either by a decline in spending or an increase in income in the household sector. Government-imposed lockdowns and quarantines and expectations of recessions may have lowered household expenditures. On the

Table 27. Average Household and Firm Sector Balances, Selected Countries
(% of GDP)

Country	Households		Firms	
	2019	2020	2019	2020
Republic of Korea	4.7	14.1	–3.1	–6.2
Spain	1.2	13.7	1.6	–1.5
United Kingdom	–0.1	10.9	–1.1	0.4
Germany	5.6	10.6	–2.4	1.2
France	2.6	9.9	–0.5	–3.1
United States	5.0	9.2	–1.4	–1.7
Netherlands	2.6	8.4	4.9	3.4
Italy	1.2	7.8	0.7	2.2
Japan	2.8	6.1	3.2	3.6
Portugal	1.4	5.6	–2.6	–4.8

GDP = gross domestic product, Q = quarter.

Notes: Ranking is based on household 2020 balances. 2020 includes only Q1 and Q2 data.

Source: Authors' calculations using flow-of funds data from CEIC and Eurostat at https://ec.europa.eu/eurostat/web/sector-accounts/data/database (accessed 1 February 2021).

Figure 18. Domestic Private Sector Balances, Selected Countries, Q1 2009–Q2 2020

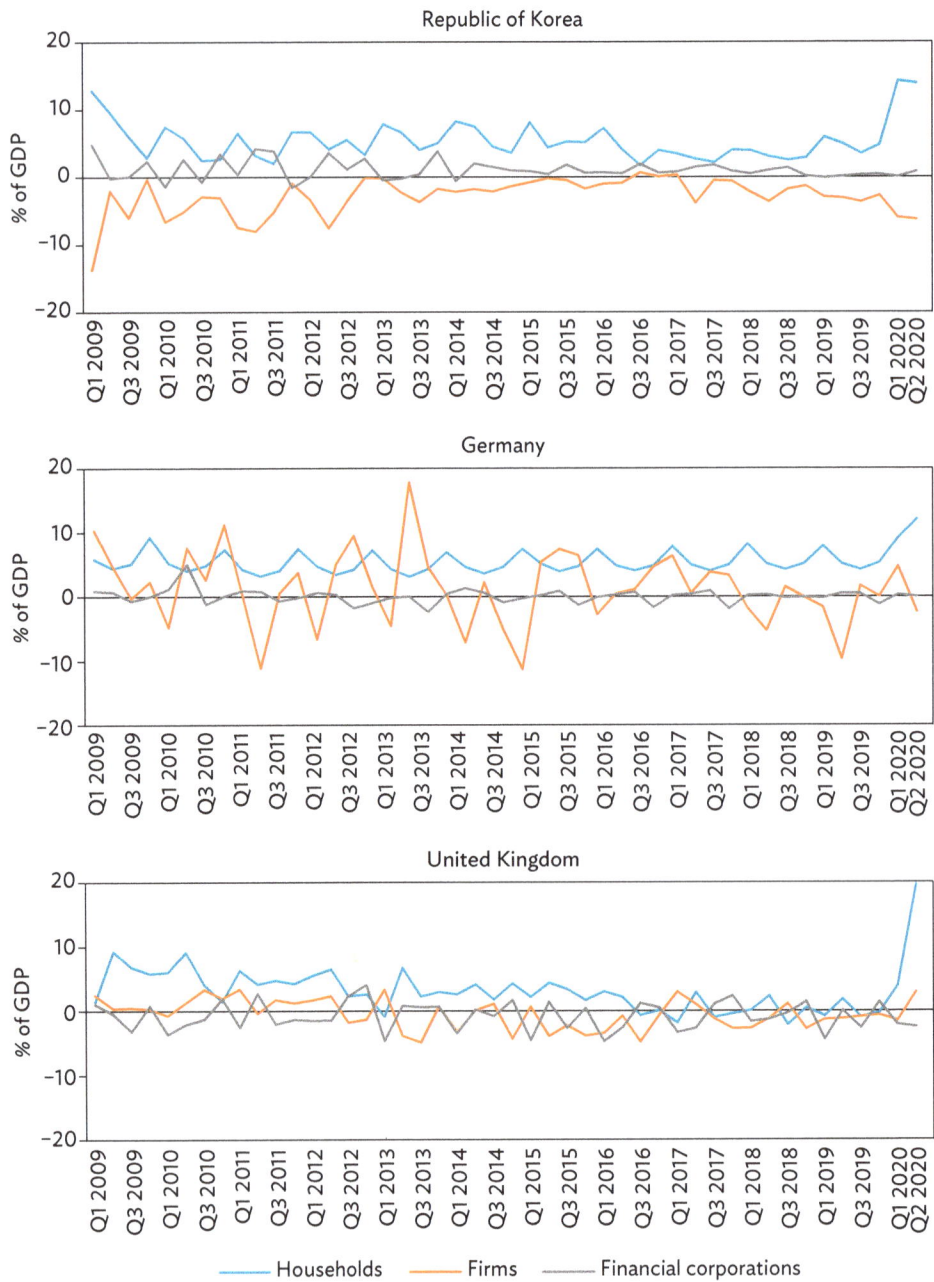

GDP = gross domestic product, Q = quarter.

Source: Authors' calculations using data from CEIC (accessed 1 February 2021).

other hand, governments have implemented economic measures to maintain or increase household income, including tax cuts, moratoria, subsidies, grants, and aids, which are under Measure 05 of the ADB COVID-19 Policy Database.

The domestic private sector balance has been a reliable indicator of financial fragility in several countries. Financial fragility refers to a worsening financial position of a household, firm, bank, government, or sector of the economy in terms of the ability of its cash inflows to service payment obligations, particularly those related to debt. The degree of financial fragility, in turn, affects the economy's risk of financial instability, whether because of greater sensitivity to shocks that affect the economy or from interactions of rising financial fragility itself with the state of the economy and/or macroeconomic policy.

In terms of the SFBs, a negative sector balance is not necessarily equivalent to increased financial fragility since the negative balance might be financed by equity (which does not carry a legal financial obligation for the issuer) or by drawing down cash or other liquid balances instead of an increase in debt and debt service obligations. However, a positive sector balance is also not necessarily equivalent to lower financial fragility.

C.   What Does It Mean if the Private Sector Financial Balance Improves Due to a Government Deficit?

In the US, increased government transfers and tightened consumer spending resulted in a spike in personal saving in 2020. A recent essay by a Federal Reserve Bank of St. Louis economist shows that net government transfers for Q2 2020 increased by 16.7% compared to the same quarter in 2019, while personal consumption expenditures declined by 9.3% (Vandenbroucke 2021, 2). The essay concludes with a chart identical to Figure 19 showing time series data for personal saving (essentially household saving) and net federal government saving, both as a percentage of GDP, noting that the two mirror each other. This observation leads the author to claim, "If U. S. households recognize that their government benefits will raise government debt and their future taxes, then they may have rationally decided to save most or all of those benefits to pay those future taxes" (Vandenbroucke 2021, 3). Economists will recognize this argument as an application of the theory of Ricardian Equivalence, whereby the private sector saves proceeds from an increase in the government deficit in anticipation of paying for an increase in future taxes.

As explained earlier in this chapter, however, the relationship between government and private sector financial positions is an accounting identity, not something that must be explained using models. Thus, the appropriate place for explaining or discussing macroeconomic outcomes is after recognizing the underlying accounting identity. The accounting identity for sector financial balances obviously holds for the US—as Figure 20 confirms—just as they do for every country. The household data in Figure 19 are simply a subset of the private sector data in Figure 20; likewise, the federal government data in Figure 19 are a subset of the total government sector data in Figure 20. Consequently, the large government deficits of 2020, particularly in the second quarter, are necessarily accompanied by an

Figure 19. Personal Saving and Net Federal Government Saving, United States, 1947–2020

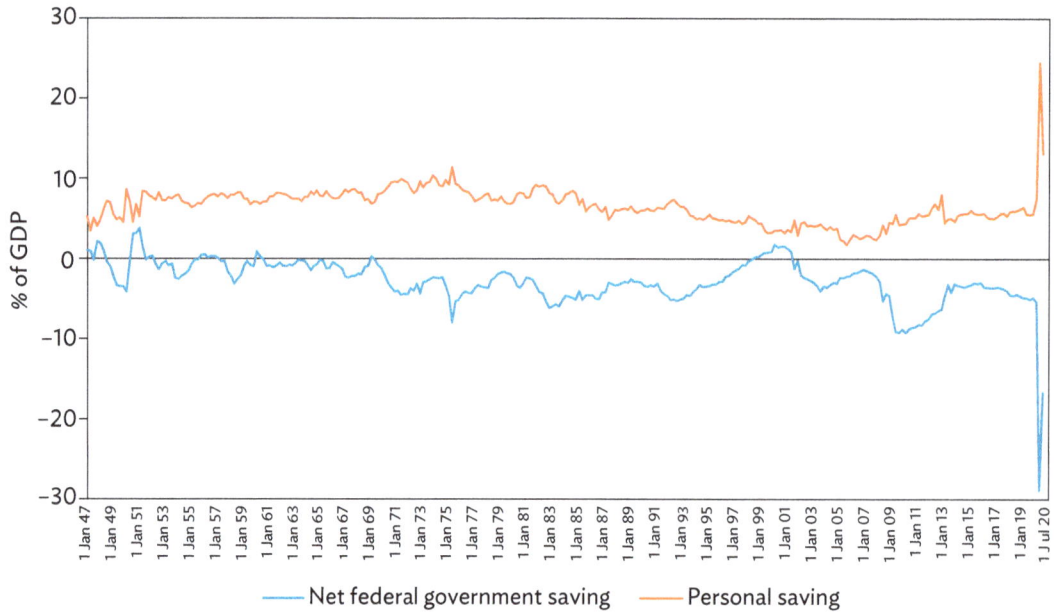

GDP = gross domestic product.

Source: Authors' calculations using United States' Flow-of-Funds Accounts at https://www.federalreserve.gov/releases/z1/ (accessed 1 February 2021).

Figure 20. Sector Financial Balances, United States, Q1 1952–Q4 2020

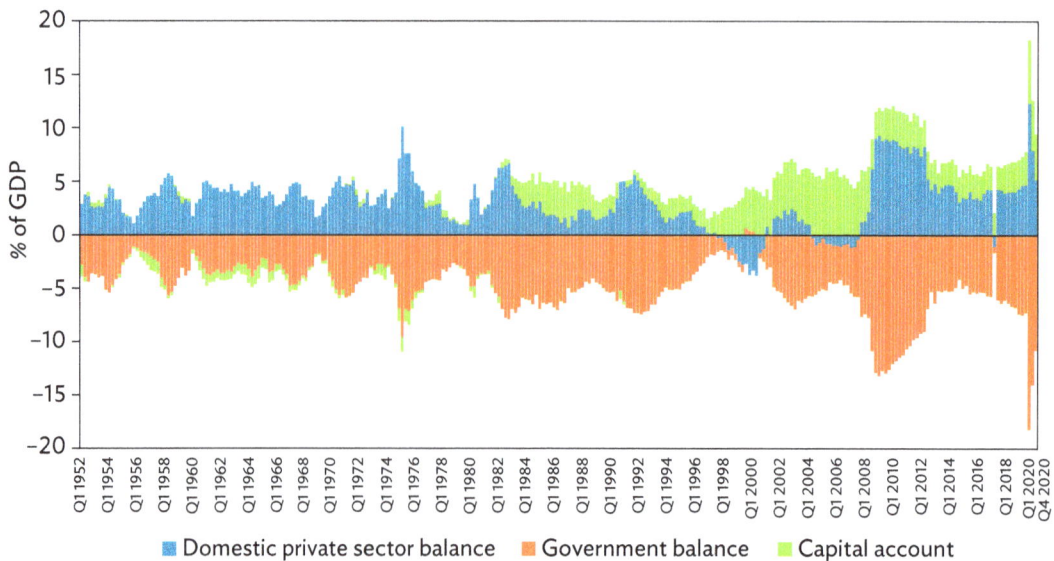

GDP = gross domestic product, Q = quarter.

Source: Authors' calculations using United States' Flow-of-Funds Accounts at https://www.federalreserve.gov/releases/z1/ (accessed 1 February 2021).

equal-sized increase in the sum of the private sector balance and the current account deficit. In this case, while both increased, the private sector balance increased more.[40]

Unlike the ROK, the US private sector balance tends to mirror the government balance, not the capital account. This is largely obvious from casual observation of Figure 20. Figure 21 isolates the federal government portion of the government balance and compares it with the private sector balance, further illustrating the historical mirroring relationship. One could predict from this relationship that the government's deficits in 2020 would mostly raise the private sector's balance.

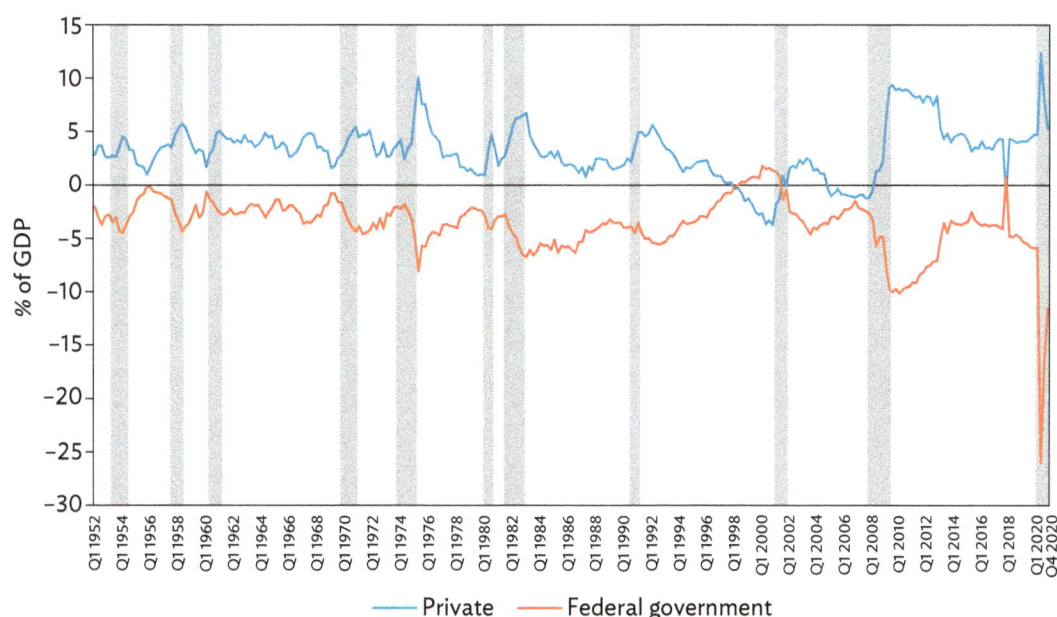

Figure 21. Private Sector and Federal Government Balances, United States, Q1 1952–Q4 2020

GDP = gross domestic product, Q = quarter.

Source: Authors' calculations using United States' Flow-of-Funds Accounts at https://www.federalreserve.gov/releases/z1/ (accessed 1 February 2021).

---

[40] The data in Figure 19 use National Income and Product Accounts, whereas the data in Figure 20 use data from Flow-of-Funds Accounts. As Box VII.1 explains, these are not necessarily the same. In particular, the household sector financial balance that is part of the private sector balance in Figure 20 and also in Figure 21 is not equivalent to "personal saving" in Figure 19.

On the other hand, historical data of the components of the private sector balance shown in Figure 22 would not necessarily suggest that the household portion of the private sector balance would dominate as it did in 2020. While previous large declines in the federal government balance, most notably during recessions (vertical gray columns in Figures 21 and 22), routinely accompanied significant increases in the household portion of the private sector balance, increases in the firm's sector's balance were just as routine. The 2020 government deficit, however, did not bring a similar increase in the firm sector balance as it did in previous recessions.

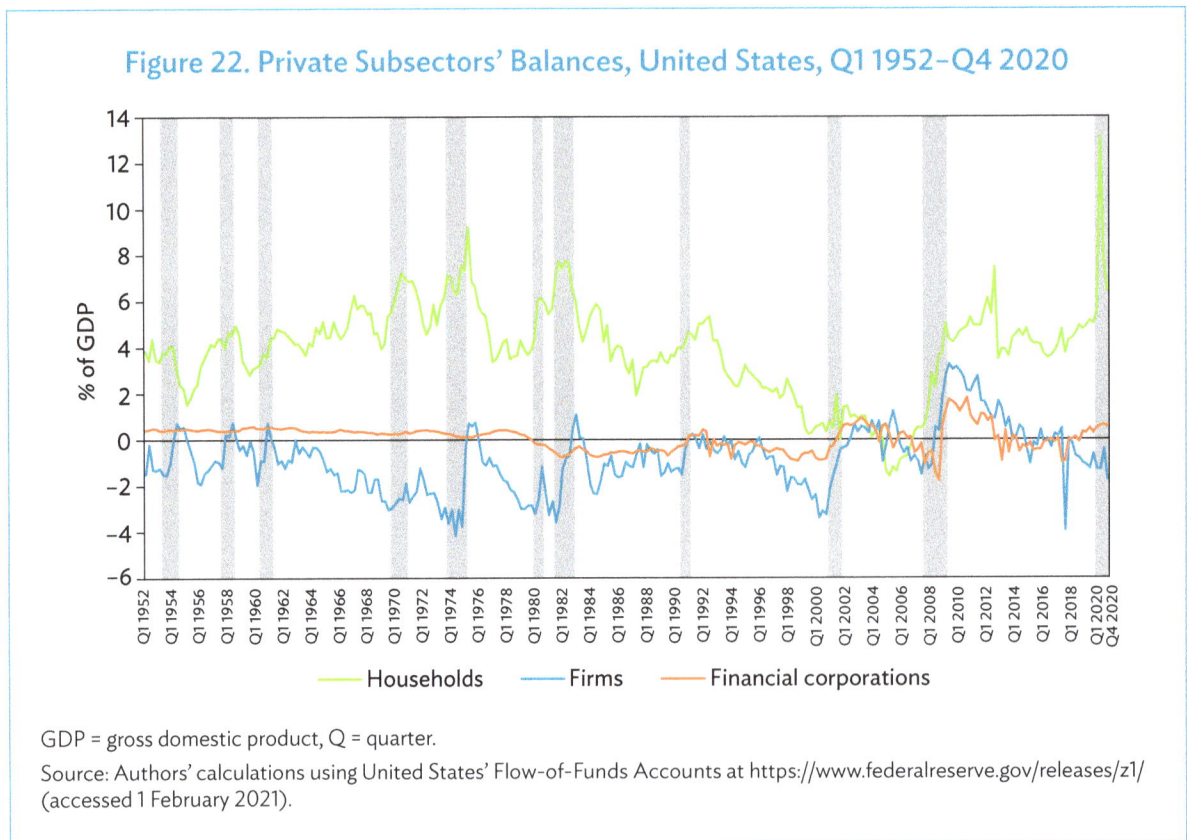

Figure 22. Private Subsectors' Balances, United States, Q1 1952–Q4 2020

GDP = gross domestic product, Q = quarter.
Source: Authors' calculations using United States' Flow-of-Funds Accounts at https://www.federalreserve.gov/releases/z1/ (accessed 1 February 2021).

Table 28 further illustrates this same point by presenting changes in the US federal government balance in the periods with significant peak-to-trough swings—all coinciding with recessions, as is visible in Figures 21 and 22—since 1974, alongside changes during these same periods in the private sector balance, broken down by households, firms, and financial sectors. In particular, prior to 2020, the nearly 40-year historical record shows that the firm balance on average rises more than the household subsector balance (3.51 percentage-point increase for the firm subsector compared to a 2.3 percentage-point increase for the household subsector). By contrast, while the Q4 2019–Q2 2020 period shows a historically large rise in the household subsector balance, the firm subsector balance declined for the first time (by 0.69 percentage points).

**Table 28. Federal Government Balance, Private Sector Balance, and Private Subsectors'
Balances as Shares of GDP during Peak-to-Trough Swings, United States**
(Change, percentage points)

Period	Federal Government Balance	Private Sector Balance	Household Subsector Balance	Firm Subsector Balance	Financial Subsector Balance
Q2 1974–Q2 1975	−6.27	7.67	2.81	4.90	−0.04
Q2 1979–Q1 1983	−4.57	5.60	2.08	4.06	−0.56
Q1 1989–Q3 1992	−2.37	2.78	1.55	1.51	−0.28
Q2 2000–Q3 2003	−6.15	6.00	0.42	2.90	1.67
Q4 2006–Q3 2009	−8.49	10.48	4.63	4.20	1.64
Average	**−5.57**	**6.52**	**2.30**	**3.51**	**0.49**
Q4 2019–Q2 2020 [a]	−20.06	7.71	8.07	−0.69	0.32

GDP = gross domestic product, Q = quarter.

[a] The state or local government balance as a share of GDP increased by 9.35 percentage points between Q4 2019 and Q2 2020. The change in the total government sector balance as a share of GDP was −10.71 percentage points for this period.

Source: Authors' calculations using United States' Flow-of-Funds Accounts at https://www.federalreserve.gov/releases/z1/ (accessed 1 February 2021).

In other words, whereas the private sector balance increased with the fall in the government sector balance during Q4 2019–Q2 2020—as necessitated by the accounting identity absent a rise in the current account balance—what is surprising is not that the household subsector balance increased but rather that its rise accounted for all of the rise in the private sector balance. In all previous peak-to-trough swings, the firm subsector balance had also increased, usually by more than the household subsector. During Q4 2019–Q2 2020, however, the firm subsector balance declined. Note that this contradicts Vandenbroucke's (2021) Ricardian Equivalence-based interpretation of the rise in household personal saving since, if true, it should apply also to the behavior of firms. That is, Vandenbroucke (2021) gives no explanation for why only households should expect higher taxes in the future and not firms as well. As such, his argument provides no rationale for why households would save more in response to a deficit and why firms would instead do the opposite, particularly given that expected forgiveness in Payroll Protection Program loans to businesses is a significant contributor to multiple rounds of the fiscal response to COVID-19.[41]

If households were not saving government transfers in anticipation of higher taxes in the future, why did they save more? Table 29 presents monthly changes in household income, saving, spending, and employment from February 2020 to December 2020 compared to 12 months earlier, as an attempt to isolate COVID-19-related differences. Column A shows the changes in government transfers, which peaked in April 2020 due mostly to the direct payments and additional unemployment benefits provided by the CARES Act. Thereafter, the rise in transfers tapers off until falling by nearly half in

---

[41] In Figure 18, a similar decline occurs in the firm sector balance in 2020 for the ROK and Germany, although both the household and firm sector balances increased in the UK.

August 2020, and then continues to decline during the last quarter of the year. Disposable income in column B follows a similar pattern of increases and decreases, although the April and May 2020 increases are about 20%–25% smaller than the increases in government transfers. Personal saving (column C) also follows a similar pattern except that its increases are larger than the rise in government transfers (44% larger than transfers on average, in fact, for April through December 2020).

Table 29. Household Income, Saving, Spending, and Employment, United States, 2020
(Change from 12 months earlier)

	Government Transfers (A)	Disposable Personal Income (B)	Personal Saving (C)	Consumption (D)	Wages and Salaries (E)	Employment (F)
Month	$ billion					Million
February	10.7	52.5	–1.0	53.4	35.9	2.4
March	16.4	26.7	69.9	–41.0	5.8	0.6
April	290.9	233.0	432.3	–194.3	–51.3	–20.3
May	196.8	158.2	276.7	–110.6	–28.3	–17.6
June	151.3	134.4	188.1	–45.1	–11.9	–12.9
July	145.6	139.9	180.3	–32.3	–2.8	–11.3
August	82.3	84.2	113.1	–21.1	2.6	–10.0
September	79.3	91.3	105.1	–7.5	8.3	–9.5
October	58.4	76.1	92.6	–9.2	10.2	–9.0
November	47.5	48.8	75.6	–18.3	9.8	8.9
December	54.0	57.2	93.5	–26.7	11.7	–9.3

Source: Authors' calculations using United States National Income and Product Accounts at https://fred.stlouisfed.org/tags/series?t=bea%3Bnipa (accessed 1 February 2021).

This much larger rise in personal saving obviously suggests that households have a motivation beyond saving transfers to pay taxes later or simply putting aside additional income they don't need. The decline in consumption in column D follows a pattern mirroring the rise in government transfers, but of a much smaller magnitude than the transfers: the consumption spending declines in April and May 2020, for instance, are 33% and 44% smaller than the increases in government transfers, respectively (the average for April through December 2020 is a 35% smaller decline in consumption relative to the rise in government transfers). In other words, households were saving considerably more than the rise in transfers, while reducing consumption *less* than the rise in transfers.

Columns E and F provide some explanation for this. Between April and July 2020, wages and salaries received by households were lower than 12 months earlier, with the largest declines in April and May. Likewise, 20 million jobs were lost in April, with only 11 million regained by the end of

December 2020. Households clearly had reasons to be concerned about their future labor income and to increase precautionary saving.

Table 30 provides additional rationale for the rise in personal saving and fall in consumption. The first three rows show quarterly changes from 12 months earlier in the three consumption categories—durables, nondurables, and services. All three declined in Q2 2020, but it is clear that the decline in services throughout the year, starting in March, is driving the fall in consumption spending. The final five rows of Table 30 show four of the major subcategories of spending on services—health-care services, transportation services, recreational services, and food services and accommodations—and the total across all four subcategories. The total shows that the decline in services consumption is roughly the same as the decline in spending in the four subcategories. It is well known that each of these four subcategories were greatly affected by COVID-19-related restrictions, lockdowns, and so forth.[42] In short, in addition to the precautionary reasons for reducing consumption, households further reduced purchases when services (and goods, particularly in Q2 2020) became unavailable for purchase.

Table 30. Consumer Spending by Category, United States
(Change from 12 months earlier, $ billion)

Category	Q1 2020	Q2 2020	Q3 2020	Q4 2020
Durables	1	–14	50	49
Nondurables	34	–25	29	25
Services	33	–311	–140	–128
Health-care services	–1	–110	–22	–13
Transportation services	–4	–48	–32	–32
Recreational services	–9	–72	–47	–46
Food services and accommodations	–13	–96	–46	–49
Total of the four service subcategories	–27	–326	–147	–140

Q = quarter.

Source: Authors' calculations using United States National Income and Product Accounts at https://fred.stlouisfed.org/tags/series?t=bea%3Bnipa (accessed 1 February 2021).

Finally, official measures of saving do not distinguish between the accumulation of additional financial wealth (for instance, net additions to balances in savings accounts or investment portfolios) and reducing financial obligations (that is, paying down household debt). According to the Federal Reserve Bank of New York's quarterly household debt and credit report, households reduced total

42   As Coombs (2020) reports, "State and federal officials ordered hospitals and physicians to curtail nonemergency care last month [March 2020] to focus on responding to coronavirus cases and to reduce the risk of patient infections in doctors' offices. Despite a surge in the use of telemedicine, the massive pullback in services late in the quarter hit the healthcare sector hard, with hospitals, outpatient surgical centers and doctor's offices all reporting big losses and cutting jobs as revenues dried up."

debt in Q2 2020 by $34 billion, which included reductions of $11 billion in debt from home equity lines of credit, $3 billion in auto loans, and $76 billion in credit card loans, but were partially offset by a $63 billion increase in mortgage debt due to historically low interest rates for those with high credit ratings. Again, given the uncertain outlook for income and employment in the first weeks and months of the COVID-19 pandemic, it is reasonable for households to reduce their debts or avoid taking on new debt.

Overall, the sector financial balances accounting identity always holds. A government sector deficit results in an identical increase in the sum of the private sector surplus and capital account. Starting there—as opposed to starting from the Ricardian Equivalence perspective—suggests a deeper look into the changes in spending, saving, and debt accumulation throughout the private sector. What emerges is that the lack of improvement in the firm subsector balance is the historically anomalous outcome, not the fact that personal saving increased as the federal government incurred large deficits. Households reduced spending and also temporarily reduced debt due to lost employment and unprecedented uncertainty of near-term employment and income prospects, and also because many services and some goods became unavailable to purchase, not due to anticipation of higher future taxes.

Even so, asking why the household and firm subsectors acted as they did is merely an intermediate step toward understanding how the sector financial balances evolved. For the study to be of full use to policy makers requires integrating the information so far with an analysis of how well policy responses to the COVID-19 pandemic—government deficits and otherwise—sustained or (even better) improved private sector financial positions relative to where they stood at the start of the pandemic. This is the subject of the next section.

D.   Domestic Private Sector Financial Position during the Pandemic

Examining the financial position of the private sector is the final step to understanding the sector's financial fragility, having started with an overall view given by SFBs and flow-of-funds data. To measure financial fragility, two types of measures (at least) are necessary—stock measures of financial obligations (expected or outstanding), and flow measures that compare cash inflows (or sources) against current or near-term payment commitments and other essential cash outflows (or uses). The former relate to financial leverage, which is usually measured using debt-to-asset or asset-to-equity (or net worth) ratios. The latter refer to the ability of the household or business to survive financially—a "financial survival constraint," in other words. For example, for the household sector, uses of funds may include mortgage/rent payments, debt service, utilities, food, transportation, and other necessities, while for the business sector, uses of funds may include variable and fixed costs, leases, principal and interest payments, taxes, and net working capital.

Using these two types of measures, the evolution of the sector's financial position and fragility can be illustrated using Figure 23. The vertical axis shows the degree or amount of leverage, while the horizontal axis shows the degree to which the financial survival constraint is relaxed (left) or tight (right). Financial positions become more fragile as they move to the north or the east of the graph, with the most fragile positions in the northeast corner. The opposite—robust or resilient financial positions—occurs as financial positions move to the south or the west of the map, with the most robust or resilient positions in the southwest corner.

Figure 23. The Financial Positions Map

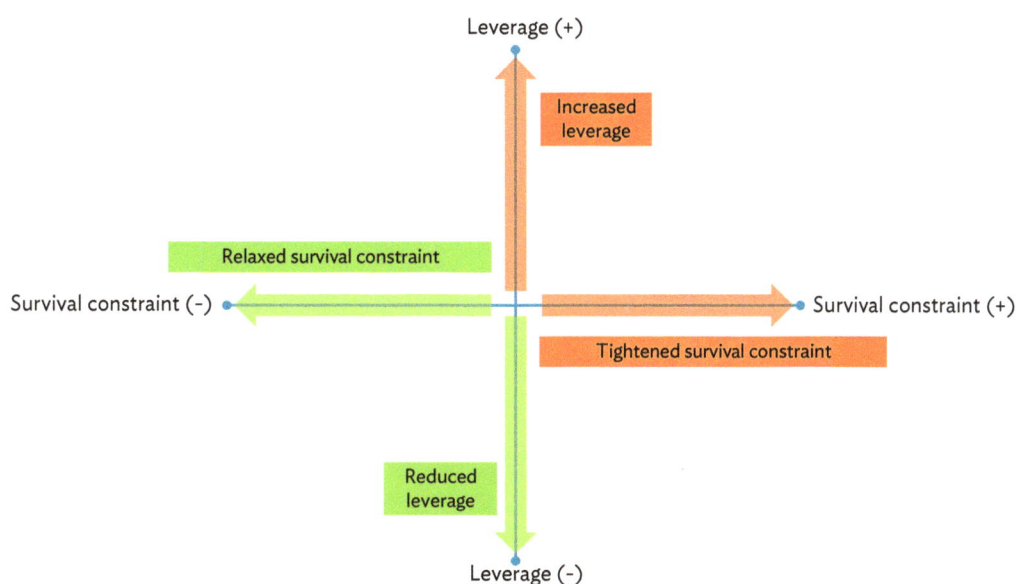

Source: Authors' illustration.

The initial impact of the pandemic on private sector financial positions can be described by looking at the two measures of financial fragility. The shock resulted in collapsing income and revenues while most debt service, rent, utilities, and other payment commitments remained the same. Regardless of the private sector's starting financial position, the economic shutdown tightened the sector's financial survival constraint and shifted its position further to the right of financial fragility map. The shock, in turn, increases the credit risks of the private sector, which raises the interest rate on refinancing short-term commitments, if available. Lower net worth and higher interest rates, if part of the refinancing, can raise leverage, which results in an upward shift in the financial fragility map. This financial position evolution in response to a pandemic shock is illustrated in Figure 24.

Because the private sector's financial fragility may feed into the total economy's financial instability, governments ought to protect the private sector's financial position. Governments' response at the onset of the pandemic shock, if adequate, should have protected the private sector by preventing or delaying increased leverage and easing its financial survival constraint.

Figure 24. Evolution of the Private Sector's Financial Position after a Pandemic Shock

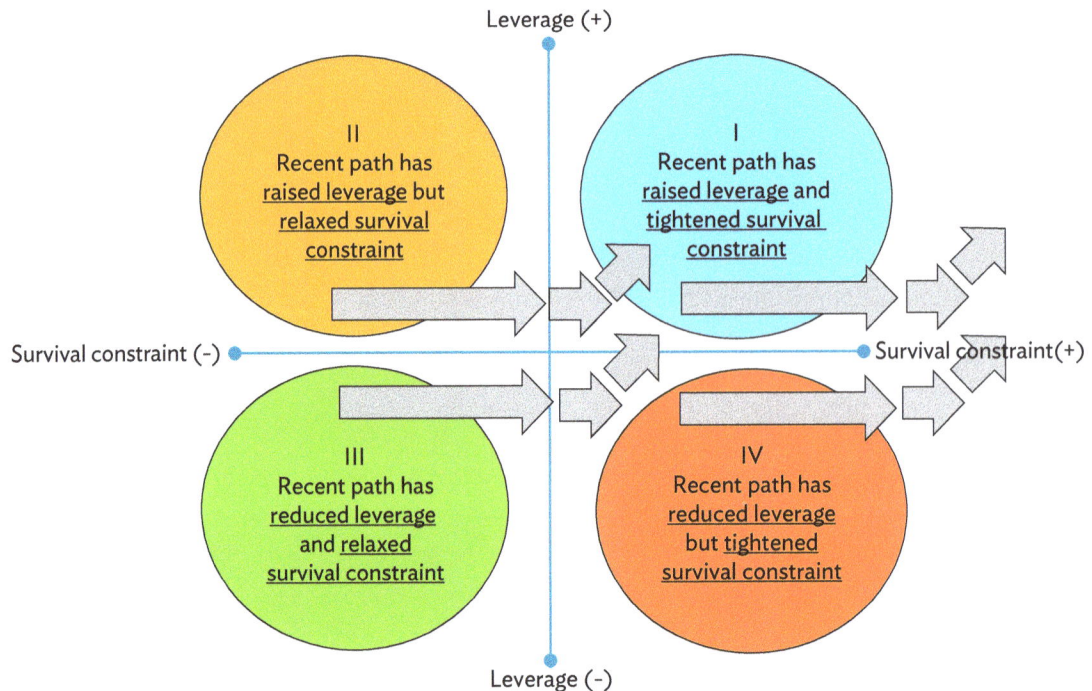

Leverage (+)

II
Recent path has
<u>raised leverage</u> but
<u>relaxed survival constraint</u>

I
Recent path has
<u>raised leverage</u> and
<u>tightened survival constraint</u>

Survival constraint (−) ●————————————————————● Survival constraint(+)

III
Recent path has
<u>reduced leverage</u>
and <u>relaxed survival constraint</u>

IV
Recent path has
<u>reduced leverage</u>
but <u>tightened survival constraint</u>

Leverage (−)

Note: The gray arrows illustrate how an economic shutdown can shift the private sector's financial position upward and further to the right of the financial fragility map regardless of its starting position.
Source: Authors' illustration.

Figure 25 shows the historical trend in nonfinancial sector debt levels since 1999. From 1999 and leading up to the 2008 GFC, advanced economies had steady increases in private sector debt levels. For emerging market economies, the increases happened after the GFC. In 2020, steep increases in private sector debt levels were observed in both advanced and emerging economies. By Q2 2020, advanced economies' credit to the nonfinancial sector reached 174% of GDP, while emerging market economies' credit to the nonfinancial sector was 154% of GDP. It is important to note that because debt is measured as a share of GDP, these increases can be driven by either increases in the absolute amount of debt or decreases in GDP.

Figure 25. Credit to Nonfinancial Sector as a Percentage of Gross Domestic Product, Q1 1999–Q2 2020

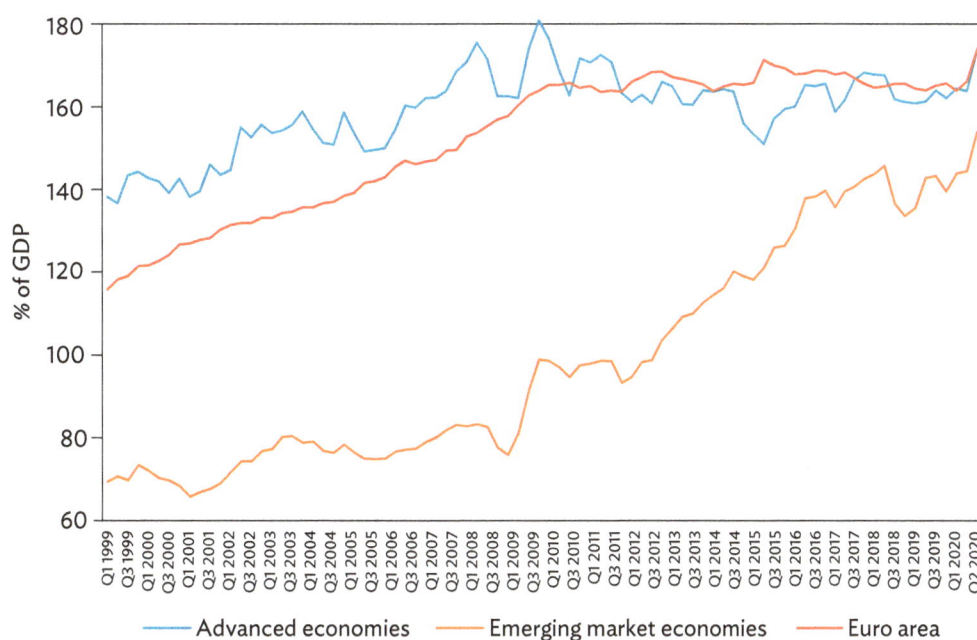

GDP = gross domestic product, Q = quarter.

Source: Bank for International Settlements. https://www.bis.org/statistics/totcredit.htm and https://www.bis.org/statistics/dsr.htm (accessed 1 February 2021).

Using data from the Bank for International Settlements, the study used proxies to measure the private sector's leverage and financial survival constraint and to plot the economies in the financial fragility map. For leverage, the study used change in the private sector's debt-to-GDP ratio as a proxy. While GDP is not the same as net worth, it can be used to scale debt. For the financial survival constraint, the analysis used change in the private sector's debt service-to-GDP ratio as a proxy. GDP scales debt service and is also an income flow. However, debt service is a narrower measure of uses of funds in determining survival constraint. In other words, actual survival constraints are likely tighter as measured by debt service ratios. Figure 26 presents the evolution of the private sector's financial position for selected developing and developed economies. The horizontal and vertical axes are the year-on-year changes in private debt service ratio and credit to the nonfinancial sector as a percentage of GDP, respectively.

As shown in Figure 26, except for Indonesia, the sample of economies shifted further in the first quadrant of the financial fragility map by Q2 2020. This meant that both measures of financial fragility increased in the early stage of the pandemic. As compared to Q1 2020, significant jumps in both measures were observed in Japan, Malaysia, the ROK, Thailand, and the UK during Q2 2020. Even for the US, financial positions remained in the first quadrant despite the reduced size of increases in the debt service ratio, which was in part due to temporary forbearances for student loans and credit card loans, and temporarily relaxed conditions for mortgage payment delinquencies. In addition to the

Figure 26. Evolution of the Private Sector's Financial Position in Selected Economies, Q1 2015–Q2 2020
(Percentage points)

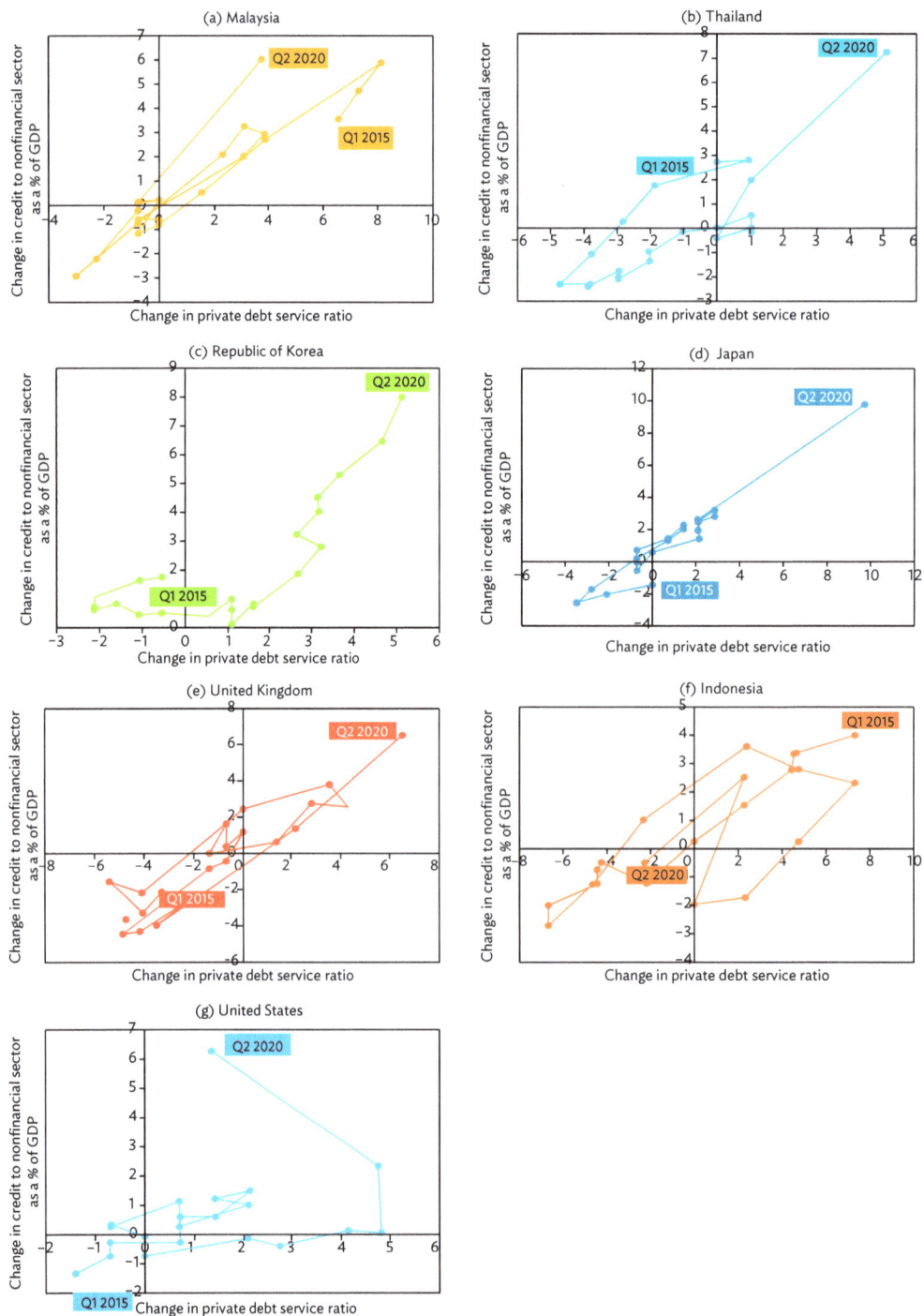

GDP = gross domestic product, Q = quarter.

Source: Authors' calculations using Bank for International Settlements data at https://www.bis.org/statistics/totcredit.htm and https://www.bis.org/statistics/dsr.htm (accessed 1 February 2021).

reasons provided, the rise in leverage can be explained partly by the reduced interest rates and relaxed oversight by financial regulators to encourage private credit creation.

E.   Conclusions

The analysis in this chapter of private financial positions during the COVID-19 pandemic yields several conclusions. At the most macro-level view given by sector financial balances, a clear pattern across economies emerged in the first half of 2020: large private sector surpluses generated by large government deficits. For most countries, current account surpluses declined as global trade slowed, and those that normally generated private sector surpluses through current account surpluses shifted to doing so through government deficits instead. Within the private sector, the countries for which information is available show that most of the increase in private sector balances came from a large increase in household balances. Whereas some have argued that households (in this case, in the US) were simply saving the increased government transfers rather than spending them, possibly in anticipation of higher taxes, the reality is that (a) households increased saving by far more than the rise in government transfers, (b) households increased saving mostly by reducing purchases of services that were unavailable for purchase and perhaps out of precautionary reasons due to potential income and/or job loss, and (c) nonfinancial firms' subsector balances fell despite rising with household balances in previous recessions. Further analysis shows that private sector financial positions in terms of debt ratios and debt service ratios worsened in early 2020, which is atypical for the private sector in recessions (although Indonesia may be an exception since it showed improvements in both private sector debt and debt service ratios). Whether government policies and interventions were enough to protect the private sector's financial position during the pandemic is still a continuing question. However, in several cases, large private sector surpluses accompanied significant increases in private debt and debt service ratios, which suggests that in these cases, the government deficits driving the large increases in private sector financial positions may not have been large enough to return private financial positions to pre-pandemic levels. With continued lockdowns and new waves of infection throughout 2020, incomes and balance sheets of the households and firms may continue to worsen.

References

Accountant-General's Department. 2019 [update]. *Understanding Singapore Government's Borrowing and Its Purposes—An Overview.* Singapore: Ministry of Finance.

Asian Development Bank (ADB). ADB COVID-19 Policy Database. https://covid19policy.adb.org.

————. *Asian Development Outlook (ADO) 2020.* Database for Cook Islands (accessed 15 April 2020).

Bangko Sentral ng Pilipinas. 2016. *Revised Framework for Monetary Operations Under the BSP Interest Rate Corridor (IRC) System.* Manila.

————. 2020. "BSP to Remit P20 Billion Dividends to Fight COVID-19." Media Release. 26 March.

Bank for International Settlements. Credit to the non-financial sector. https://www.bis.org/statistics/totcredit.htm (accessed 1 February 2021).

————. Debt service ratios for the private non-financial sector. https://www.bis.org/statistics/dsr.htm (accessed 1 February 2021).

Barbosa-Filho, Nelson H. 2018. "A Vertical Social Accounting Matrix of the U.S. Economy." *Journal of Post Keynesian Economics* 41 (4): 578–97. https://doi.org/10.1080/01603477.2018.1486208.

Battersby, Bryn, W. Raphael Lam, and Elif Ture. 2020. "Tracking the $9 Trillion Global Fiscal Support to Fight COVID-19." https://blogs.imf.org/2020/05/20/tracking-the-9-trillion-global-fiscal-support-to-fight-covid-19/.

Center for Systems Science and Engineering at Johns Hopkins University. COVID-19 Data Repository. https://github.com/CSSEGISandData/COVID-19 (accessed 27 April 2020).

Coombs, Bertha. 2020. "Plunge in Health-Care Spending a Big Reason US Economy Sank in First Quarter." CNBC.com (April 29). https://www.cnbc.com/2020/04/29/plunge-in-health-care-spending-a-big-reason-us-economy-sank-in-first-quarter.html.

Duffie, Darrell. 2020. "Still the World's Safe Haven? Redesigning the U.S. Treasury Market after the COVID-19 Crisis." Hutchins Center Working Paper No. 62 (June). Washington, DC: The Brookings Institute.

European Center for Disease Prevention and Control (ECDC). Data on the Geographic Distribution of COVID-19 Cases Worldwide. https://www.ecdc.europa.eu/en/publications-data/download-todays-data-geographic-distribution-covid-19-cases-worldwide (accessed 27 April–14 December 2020).

Eurostat. https://ec.europa.eu/eurostat/web/sector-accounts/data/database (accessed 1 February 2021).

Felipe, Jesus, and Scott Fullwiler. 2020a. "ADB COVID-19 Policy Database: A Guide." *Asian Development Review* 37 (2): 1–20.

_____. 2020b. "The PRC's Monetization Debate." Presentation at the Asian Development Bank. 24 July.

Fleming, Michael. 2020. "Treasury Market Liquidity and the Federal Reserve during the COVID-19 Pandemic." *Liberty Street Economics*. 29 May.

Government of Singapore Investment Corporation (GIC). https://www.gic.com.sg/faq/ (accessed 30 September 2020).

He, Zengping, and Genliang Jia. 2020. "An Institutional Analysis of China's Reform of Their Monetary Policy Framework." *Journal of Economic Issues* 54 (3): 838–54.

International Monetary Fund (IMF). Global Debt Database. Central Government Debt. https://www.imf.org/external/datamapper/CG_DEBT_GDP@GDD/SWE (accessed 4 January 2021).

_____. *World Economic Outlook (WEO) Database*, April 2020. https://www.imf.org/external/pubs/ft/weo/2020/01/weodata/index.aspx (accessed 3 April 2020).

Kelton [Bell], Stephanie. 2000. "Do Taxes and Bonds Finance Government Spending?" *Journal of Economic Issues* 34 (3): 603–20.

Kurohi, Rei. 2020. "Singapore's Revenue Position Set to Remain Weak for Some Time." *The Straits Times*. 6 October.

Lavoie, Marc, and Peng Wang. 2012. "The 'Compensation Thesis,' as Exemplified by the Case of the Chinese Central Bank." *International Review of Applied Economics* 23 (3): 287–301.

Leyco, Chino S. 2020. "BSP Extends Zero-Interest Loans to Government." *Manila Bulletin*. 30 March.

Liu, Shangxi. 2020. "Opinion—Deficit Monetization Is a Reasonable Choice for the Current Fiscal and Monetary Policy Combination." *Caixin*. 14 May (original in Chinese).

Logan, Lorie K. 2020. "The Federal Reserve's Market Functioning Purchases: From Supporting to Sustaining." Remarks at a Securities Industry and Financial Markets Association webinar. 15 July.

Ma, Jun. 2020. "My View on Monetization of Fiscal Deficit." *Financial News*. 18 May (original in Chinese).

Martin, Antoine, and James McAndrews. 2008. "Should There Be Intraday Money Markets?" Federal Reserve Bank of New York Staff Report No. 337.

Monetary Authority of Singapore. MAS Standing Facility. https://www.mas.gov.sg/monetary-policy/liquidity-facilities/mas-standing-facility (accessed 1 October 2020).

_____. 2013. *Monetary Policy Operations in Singapore*. Monetary and Domestic Markets Management Department. March.

_____. 2014. *MAS Notice 758—Minimum Cash Balance.* Revised on 6 March.

_____. 2018. *Frequently Asked Questions on Singapore's Monetary Policy Framework.* Economic Policy Group. 10 October.

Noble, Luz Wendy T. 2020. "BSP Can Lend More to Government under Bayanihan II." *Business World.* 15 September.

Parenteau, Rob. 2010. "On Fiscal Correctness and Animal Sacrifices." https://www.nakedcapitalism.com/2010/03/parenteau-on-fiscal-correctness-and-animal-sacrifices-leading-the-piigs-to-slaughter-part-1.html (accessed 1 February 2021).

People's Bank of China (PBoC). 2020. Open Market Operations No. 124 [2020]. http://www.pbc.gov.cn/en/3688229/3688335/3730267/4046489/index.html.

Pozsar, Zoltan. 2019a. "Collateral Supply and O/N Rates." *Global Money Notes #22.* Investment Strategy Department, Credit Suisse AG. 31 May.

_____. 2019b. "Design Options for an O/N Repo Facility." *Global Money Notes #25.* Investment Strategy Department, Credit Suisse AG. 9 September.

Raju, Manu, and Clare Foran. 2020. "Hill Leaders Reach $900 Billion Covid Relief Deal in Breakthrough following Partisan Disputes." *CNN.* 20 December. https://edition.cnn.com/2020/12/20/politics/stimulus-latest-shutdown-deadline.

Segal, Stephanie, and Gerstel Dylan. 2020. "Breaking Down the G20 COVID-19 Fiscal Response: May 2020 Update." https://www.csis.org/analysis/breaking-down-g20-covid-19-fiscal-response-may-2020-update.

Singapore Ministry of Finance. n.d. Our Nation's Reserves. https://tinyurl.com/453fwvtk (accessed on 1 August 2020).

Tymoigne, Eric. 2014. "Modern Money Theory and Interrelations between the Treasury and the Central Bank—The Case of the United States." *Journal of Economic Issues* 48 (3): 641–62.

Vandenbroucke, Guillaume. 2021. "Personal Saving during the COVID-19 Recession." *Economic Synopses* 2021 (2). https://doi.org/10.20955/es.2021.2.

World Bank. World Development Indicators (WDI). https://databank.worldbank.org/source/world-development-indicators (accessed 4 January 2021).

Worldometer. Reported Cases and Deaths by Country, Territory, or Conveyance. https://www.worldometers.info/coronavirus/ (accessed 19 December 2020).

Wu, Xiaoling. 2020. "Analysis of China's Fiscal Deficit Monetization." *Financial News.* 18 May (original in Chinese).

www.ingramcontent.com/pod-product-compliance
Lightning Source LLC
Chambersburg PA
CBHW042033220326
41599CB00045BA/7289